David Keen

The Economic Functions of Violence in Civil Wars

Adelphi Paper 320

Oxford University Press, Great Clarendon Street, Oxford OX2 6DP

Oxford New York

Athens Auckland Bangkok Bombay Calcutta Cape Town
Dar es Salaam Delhi Florence Hong Kong Istanbul Karachi
Kuala Lumpur Madras Madrid Melbourne Mexico City
Nairobi Paris Singapore Taipei Tokyo Toronto
and associated companies in
Berlin Ibadan

Oxford is a trade mark of Oxford University Press

Published in the United States
by Oxford University Press Inc., New York

© The International Institute for Strategic Studies 1998

First published June 1998 by **Oxford University Press** for
The International Institute for Strategic Studies
23 Tavistock Street, London WC2E 7NQ

Director John Chipman
Editor Gerald Segal
Assistant Editor Matthew Foley
Design and Production Mark Taylor

British Library Cataloguing in Publication Data
Data available

Library of Congress Cataloguing in Publication Data

ISBN 0-19-922373-4
ISSN 0567-932X

contents

maps

glossary

ADFL	Alliance of Democratic Forces for the Liberation of Congo-Zaire
ANC	African National Congress (South Africa)
BP	British Petroleum
BRA	Bougainville Revolutionary Army
CRA	*Co-ordination de la Résistance Armée* (Niger)
CSNPD	*Comité de Sursaut National pour la Paix et la Démocratie* (Chad)
DROC	Democratic Republic of Congo (former Zaire)
ECOMOG	West African Cease-fire Monitoring Group
ELN	*Ejército de Liberación Nacional* (Colombia)
EO	Executive Outcomes
EZLN	*Ejército Zapatista de Liberación Nacional* (Mexico)
FADH	*Forces Armées d'Haiti*
FAR	Rwandan Armed Forces
FARC	*Fuerzas Armadas Revolucionarias de Colombia*
FARF	*Forces Armées de la République Fédérale* (Chad)
FDD	Front for the Defence of Democracy (Burundi)
FDR	*Front Démocratique de Renouveau* (Niger)
FIS	*Front Islamique de Salut* (Algeria)
FLN	*Front pour la Libération Nationale* (Algeria)
Frelimo	*Frente para a Libertaçao de Moçambique*
FRETILIN	*Frente Revolucionario Timorense de Libertação e Independência* (East Timor)
GIA	*Groupe Islamique Armée* (Algeria)
ICRC	International Committee of the Red Cross
IMT	Islamic Movement of Tajikistan
IRA	Irish Republican Army
KDPI	Kurdish Democratic Party of Iran

KNU	Karen National Union (Myanmar)
LRA	Lord's Resistance Army (Uganda)
LTTE	Liberation Tigers of Tamil Eelam (Sri Lanka)
Me–K	*Mujahidin-e-Khalq* (Iran)
MFDC	*Mouvement des Forces Démocratiques de la Casamance* (Senegal)
MFUA	*Mouvements et Fronts Unifiés de l'Azouad* (Mali)
MILF	Moro Islamic Liberation Front (Philippines)
MNLF	Moro National Liberation Front (Philippines)
MPLA	*Movimento Popular de Libertaçao de Angola*
MRTA	*Movimiento Revolucionario Túpac Amaru* (Peru)
NCGUB	National Coalition Government of the Union of Burma
NGO	Non-governmental organisation
NLF	National Liberation Front (Viet Cong)
NPA	New People's Army (Philippines)
NPF	National Patriotic Front (Liberia)
ORA	*Organisation de la Résistance Armée* (Niger)
PA	Palestinian Authority
PKK	Kurdistan Workers' Party (Turkey)
PLO	Palestine Liberation Organisation
POLISARIO	*Frente Popular para la Liberación de Saguia el-Hamra y de Río de Oro* (Western Sahara)
Renamo	*Resistência Nacional Moçambicana* (Mozambique)
RPA	Rwandan Patriotic Army
RUF	Revolutionary United Front (Sierra Leone)
SL	*Sendero Luminoso* (Peru)
SLA	South Lebanon Army
SNM	Somali National Movement
SPDC	State Peace and Development Council (Myanmar)
SPLA	Sudan People's Liberation Army
UCK	Kosovo Liberation Army (Federal Republic of Yugoslavia)
UNDP	UN Development Programme
UNITA	*União Nacional para a Independência Total de Angola*
UNOSOM	UN Operation in Somalia
UNTAC	UN Transitional Authority in Cambodia
URNG	*Unidad Revolucionaria Nacional Guatemalteca* (Guatemala)

Rumours of the death of civil wars have been greatly exaggerated. There were grounds for optimism as the Cold War ended amid talk of a 'New World Order', with a fresh potential for international co-operation apparently exemplified by the 1991 Gulf War. The majority of civil conflicts since the Second World War, from Afghanistan to Vietnam, had been fuelled by superpower rivalry and injections of arms and aid. Yet, while the old 'ideological' explanations no longer seem to apply, conflicts continue. Some have been born precisely from the demise of communist regimes in the Soviet Union and Yugoslavia; others have simply refused to end. Angola relapsed into civil war almost as soon as it had tasted peace in 1992–93.[1] In some countries war, often in the guise of 'complex emergencies', has become more normal than peace – Cold War or no Cold War.[2] Myanmar has arguably been at war with itself since 1948. Even conflicts that appeared to be resolved, such as those in Cambodia, El Salvador and Mozambique, have shown signs of intractability.[3] If the persistence of civil wars has left many analysts puzzled, so has their nature. The absence of clear political programmes, the pro-liferation of factions, disintegrating lines of command and ferocious attacks against civilians have all produced both confusion and outrage.[4]

Under these circumstances, we need a better understanding of the forces sparking and sustaining civil wars.[5] Three broad approaches to analysing civil wars stand out. The first is an essentially Cold War model, which portrays conflict as being between two sides, usually an insurrection met by a counter-insurgency. This framework appeared suitable to describe conflicts between the 1950s and the 1980s, when anti-colonial wars often ran alongside, and sometimes gave way to, revolutionary struggles. This type of analysis focuses first on background causes to explain what the war is about and who it is 'between', then on tactics and battles won and lost by either side.

Faced with conflicts that do not fit this traditional model – in Bosnia-Herzegovina, Liberia and Rwanda, for example – some analysts have sought to explain the irrationality and unpredictability of civil wars by invoking a kind of 'chaos theory'. The end of the Cold War, so the argument goes, freed tribal, ethnic and national rivalries once kept in check by strong regimes.[6] War became evil or medieval, mindless violence propelled by a witches' brew of over-population, tribalism, drug-taking and environmental decline.

The third strand of analysis emphasises war's negative consequences. This apparently common-sense approach, embraced by many UN agencies and non-governmental organisations (NGOs) and emphasised in the media, portrays conflict as disrupting the economy and interrupting 'benevolent' progress. The best response is therefore a speedy transition from wartime relief to development, often urged while fighting still rages, and the setting of goals that appear self-evidently desirable. These usually begin with the prefix 're', and include rehabilitation, reconstruction, repatriation and resettlement.

None of these approaches should be too readily dismissed. It is often forgotten that 'traditional' revolutionary and political struggles, such as those for land reform in Latin America, continue, as do conflicts between government and rebel forces. Ethnic tensions are important in many countries, while the economic devastation of war has been well documented. But these analyses take us only so far:

- the old 'ideological' struggles have undergone a major change, and we need new tools to understand them;
- the ancient-hatreds thesis risks ignoring the prosaic political and economic roots of ethnic conflict; and
- explaining the negative consequences of war does not enlighten us as to its causes.

Where no clear ideological divides can be made out, how can we explain the motivation of those who allow – even cause – a disastrous conflict? How can the ancient-hatreds analysis explain why conflict should suddenly erupt between peoples who have lived peacefully together for long periods?

Analyses that focus on destruction or ethnic hatred view conflict as a collapse or failure. But the problem of war needs to be posed in more positive terms. What use is conflict? In whose interests is it waged? Who produces violence, how, and why? This paper suggests that internal conflicts have persisted

civil wars persist partly because of rational economic calculations

not so much *despite* the intentions of rational people, as *because* of them. The apparent 'chaos' of civil war can be used to further local and short-term interests. These are frequently *economic*: to paraphrase Carl von Clausewitz, war has increasingly become the continuation of economics by other means. War is not simply a breakdown in a particular system, but a way of creating an alternative system of profit, power and even protection.

Economic interests have rarely fuelled unlimited violence. Many contemporary conflicts have been carefully contained, with only limited fighting, if not cooperation, between opposing factions. Instead, there has been a heavier emphasis on controlling production and trade, and – a related enterprise – on controlling, raiding and exploiting civilians. This cooperation is significant when considering the possibilities for peace. The distinction between war and peace may be hazy, and the two may not necessarily be opposites. War can involve cooperation between 'sides' at the expense of civilians; peace can see adversaries striking deals that institutionalise violence, corruption and exploitation. These similarities help to explain how peace can be possible, and why it has often swiftly relapsed into war.

To understand violence in civil wars, we need to understand the economics underpinning it. Conflict can create war economies, often in regions controlled by rebels or warlords and linked to international trading networks; members of armed gangs can benefit from looting; and regimes can use violence to deflect opposition, reward supporters or maintain their access to resources. Under these circumstances, ending civil wars becomes difficult. Winning may not be desirable: the point of war may be precisely the legitimacy which it confers on actions that in peacetime would be punishable as crimes. Whereas analysts have tended to assume that war is the 'end' and abuse of civilians the 'means', it is important to consider the opposite possibility: that the end is to engage in abuse or crimes that bring immediate rewards, while the means is war and its perpetuation. Rather than simply asking which groups 'support' a rebellion or counter-insurgency, it is important to ask which groups take advantage of these situations for their own purposes.

This paper distinguishes between two forms of economic violence: 'top-down', which is mobilised by political leaders and entrepreneurs; and 'bottom-up', where violence is actively embraced by 'ordinary' people, either civilians or low-ranking soldiers. Much of the violence in contemporary conflicts has been initiated not by rebels seeking to transform the state, but by élites trying to defend vested interests. Many of these élite groups gained ascendancy in post-colonial states; others enjoyed privileges under communist regimes. Both may be threatened by pressures for democracy, whether domestic or international, as well as by outright rebellion. While often amassing considerable personal wealth, these groups typically preside over states unable to fight an effective and disciplined counter-insurgency or to provide basic services to their citizens. A range of factors can contribute to top-down violence, including a weak state, an economic crisis, a strong threat to a regime and competition for valuable resources. Ordinary people, driven by fear, need or greed, may turn to violence for a solution to their economic and social problems. Bottom-up violence can be fuelled by social and economic exclusion, the absence of a strong revolutionary organisation or ideology, and the belief that violence will go unpunished.

Increasingly, civil wars that appear to have begun with political aims have mutated into conflicts in which short-term economic benefits are paramount. While ideology and identity remain important in understanding conflict, they may not tell the whole story. Portraying civil wars as simply revolutionary struggles between opposing sides obscures the emerging political economy from which the combatants can benefit. Emphasising so-called ancient ethnic hatreds offers few opportunities for policy-makers other than, perhaps, an excuse for inaction.[7] It may also disguise the role that economic and political agendas play in manipulating ethnicity. Similarly, the development approach's enthusiasm for restoring a pre-war economy fails to understand the extent to which a conflict may have been caused by precisely those pre-war conditions. To achieve more lasting solutions, we need to acknowledge that, for significant groups both at the top and at the bottom of society, violence can be an opportunity, rather than a problem. This paper suggests that taking better account of the economic agendas that can emerge in civil wars would significantly improve conflict-resolution initiatives and the effectiveness of international aid.

chapter 1

The Economic Benefits of Civil War

To understand why wars start and how they might be stopped, we need to examine the *nature* of conflict.[1] This chapter looks at two common but misleading notions: first, that conflict has only negative economic consequences for local populations; and second, that winning is the combatants' overriding aim.

Economic Agendas

'Traditional' analyses, which portray civil wars as primarily political or military struggles, tend to emphasise tactics rather than political economy. The economic benefits arising from wars may therefore be overlooked. Some economic aims can be furthered by controlling the state. Others are more immediate, and do not depend upon holding the reins of power; they usually involve breaking the law, rather than changing or preserving a system of laws. These activities fall into seven categories:

- *Pillage.* Pillaging has long been used to supplement or replace soldiers' wages.[2] In modern times, it has taken place in the Central African Republic in 1996, Zaire/Democratic Republic of Congo (DROC) since independence in 1960, and parts of Eastern Europe after the collapse of communism. Although plundering has often been seen as the work of reckless individuals, it may also be a group activity organised on a considerable scale, as with the wholesale looting of villages by Bosnian Serbs during the 1992–95 war. Pillaging may also be funded by investors. Spanish entrepreneurs financed the Conquest of the Americas in the sixteenth century.[3] In modern times, northern Sudanese cattle-merchants helped to fund large-scale looting of cattle in the south in the late 1980s.

- *Protection money.* Warlords, security personnel or mafia-type bosses may offer 'protection' from violence in return for payment. This may take place in wartime or in peace. Examples include paramilitaries in Northern Ireland, particularly the Irish Republican Army (IRA), and regional warlords in Liberia and Somalia. Iraqi prison guards have allowed inmates to escape in return for payment from relatives.[4] Protection money may also be demanded from companies: from the early 1980s, Mozambique's rebel *Resistência Nacional Moçambicana* (Renamo) movement obtained regular payments from a subsidiary of UK conglomerate Lonrho for 'protecting' the Beira oil pipeline.[5]

- *Trade.* Controlling or monopolising trade has been an important factor in civil wars in Africa, Asia and Latin America, where 'forced markets', rather than market forces, may dictate the distribution of resources.[6] War may cause price movements profitable to some, and may make it easier to threaten or constrain trading rivals. Officials may profit by allowing government restrictions on wartime trading to be breached; conflict may make it easier for warlords to avoid paying government taxes. One profitable aspect of trade may be procuring arms, which frequently involves kickbacks for local officials. The International Monetary Fund (IMF) questioned the relevance of much of the military equipment bought by the Sierra Leone military government in 1992–96.

- *Labour exploitation.* Threatening individuals or groups may force them to work cheaply or for free. In extreme cases, such as Myanmar and Sudan, conflict has allowed forms of slavery to re-emerge.

- *Land.* Conflict may depopulate large areas, allowing new groups to claim land, water and mineral resources – as in, for example, Sudan in the late 1980s. The prospect of gaining access to scarce natural resources appears to have been an important factor in encouraging factions in northern Iraq and in Somalia to cooperate with the regime in repressing neighbouring factions and clans. In Somalia in the 1980s and early 1990s, elements of the *Marehan* clan took over land in the Jubba and Shabeelle River areas, while the agricultural *Rahanweyne* were ejected.[7]

- *Stealing aid supplies.* Violence causes suffering, and may prompt foreign relief aid. It may also secure access to that aid once it arrives. Even during the Cold War, when conflicts were often fuelled by superpower rivalries, aid and military assistance created rent-seeking opportunities for local groups and strengthened their interest in perpetuating conflict.[8]

- *Benefits for the military.* Economically, the military may do better when conflict necessitates a sizeable army or justifies a role in government. Benefits may include higher salaries or a seat on the board of a private company.

Supporting the Opposition

If these short-term benefits suggest that there is more to civil wars than simply winning, so too does the prevalence and persistence of behaviour that is, in military terms, counter-productive. This can take two forms: cooperating with the 'enemy'; and mounting attacks that increase, rather than reduce, political and military opposition.

Cooperative Conflict

Opposing forces in civil wars have covertly cooperated in a variety of ways:

- avoiding pitched battles (for example, in Liberia);
- coordinating their movements in and out of villages (in Sierra Leone);
- trading arrangements (in the former Yugoslavia);

- paying ransoms for captured fighters (in Chechnya and Peru); and
- selling arms and ammunition to the other side (in Cambodia, Chechnya, Sierra Leone and Sri Lanka).

Even during the Cold War, helping 'the opposition' was not unknown. During the Vietnam War, South Vietnamese officials sold war material and food to the enemy, and members of the Viet Cong bought strategically important posts, such as that of village chief. Widespread corruption, of which these were particularly dramatic examples, undermined the credibility of the South Vietnamese regime and critically weakened its military capability.[9]

Under the US-backed Lon Nol regime in Cambodia in 1970–75, officers and regional governors profited from the sale of arms and other supplies to communist guerrillas. The benefits of US military aid were increased by adding non-existent soldiers to payrolls and even by enlisting children. As in South Vietnam, this corruption alienated civilians, attracted support for the guerrillas and demoralised rank-and-file troops, while continued US support for Lon Nol appeared to weaken the non-communist opposition.[10] The underpaid Cambodian Army's reluctance to fight Vietnamese guerrillas within its borders was one reason for US Secretary of State Henry Kissinger's decision to bomb Cambodia in 1969.[11]

Trading with the enemy continues in Cambodia. The government that emerged in 1993 from the UN's ambitious peacekeeping operation has engaged in lucrative corruption. Army officers and senior government officials have become heavily involved in the logging trade and in gem-mining. In 1994, the Defence Ministry was awarded the sole right to licence timber exports and to all the revenue received from them.[12] Large profits have also been made from manipulating government contracts and from trafficking opium and heroin from Laos to Thailand.[13] Exploiting these resources has often involved reaching agreements with the Khmer Rouge, for example on spheres of influence, while officers have reportedly sold ammunition to the rebels. Some Khmer Rouge members have been enticed into abandoning the movement in return for continued access to resources in areas under their control. Conversely, the Khmer Rouge's presence may justify Army officers' continued jurisdiction in resource-rich areas.

Army officers therefore have compelling economic reasons for portraying the conflict in Cambodia as a 'traditional' battle between government and rebel forces, and for silencing or intimidating opponents of government corruption, notably by labelling them 'rebel sympathisers'. William Shawcross observes that 'villagers or tribespeople who stand in the way of the loggers have been evicted or even murdered, and journalists who try to expose the corrupt trade in timber or in drugs are liable to be threatened if not attacked or ... assassinated'.[14]

Counter-insurgency may not be all that it appears in East Timor, where some 5,000 Indonesian troops have been deployed ostensibly to tackle several hundred insurgents from the *Frente Revolucionario Timorense de Libertação e Independência* (FRETILIN). Indonesian analysts argue that other agendas are at work. According to one, the soldiers 'get a lot of funding to be there and are concerned about the threat posed by urban, unemployed youths', rather than by FRETILIN.[15]

In Sudan, government soldiers have sold arms and ammunition on the open market, some of which will have found its way into the hands of rebels.[16] Government troops in Sierra Leone have avoided pitched battles with Revolutionary United Front (RUF) rebels, preferring instead to sell them arms, ammunition and uniforms.[17] Both government and rebel forces have threatened civilians, and some- times appear to have acted together

cooperation in making money from war

to control and partially depopulate resource-rich areas, dividing the spoils between them. Some observers – Ambrose Ganda, editor of the London-based newsletter *Focus on Sierra Leone*, for example – were disturbed by the apparent warmth between representatives of the RUF and the military government at peace talks in March 1996. In May 1997, RUF and military leaders, notwithstanding six years of apparent confrontation, combined to oust the democratically elected government of Ahmed Tejan Kabbah. Kabbah had threatened to break their control over diamond resources and to end their immunity from prosecution. Kabbah's restoration in 1998 has not ended the threat of collaboration between these military factions, with soldiers from the ousted regime attacking civilians in rural areas.

Commenting on patterns of conflict in Liberia, Stephen Ellis wrote in 1995, 'Only rarely did the militias attack each other head on. For the most part, they preyed on civilians'.[18] In the same year, UN observer Tom Porteous reported seeing Liberian faction leaders drinking together at the Africa Hotel in Monrovia while their followers appeared to be fighting each other up-country.[19] After the civil war in Angola resumed in 1992, reports emerged of trading and fraternising between *União Nacional para a Independência Total de Angola* (UNITA) rebels and government forces.[20] Members of the Algerian government appear to have colluded in the violence of extremist Islamist groups in the 1990s. During the Chechen conflict of 1994–96, a former oil trader turned rebel commander said of the Russian forces: 'The army is selling weapons, which are killing its own men. But the soldiers are fully aware that the top leadership is making huge amounts of money from this war, so they are too.'[21]

Latin America is not exempt from 'cooperative conflict' of this kind. Some 40,000 Guatemalan soldiers, plus around 500,000 members of Army-backed 'civil patrols', failed to bring under control the 2,000-strong *Unidad Revolucionaria Nacional Guatemalteca* (URNG) rebel group until 1994, despite the fact that it had not posed a major threat to the government since the mid-1980s.[22] In Peru, the Army, supposedly tasked with suppressing the drugs trade and *Sendero Luminoso* (SL) guerrillas, has tolerated – even 'taxed' – drug shipments. Senior Army and police officers in Tocache in northern Peru were earning up to $5,000 a flight on shipments of coca paste, estimated to have accounted for 20% of world supply, in the early 1990s.[23] Officers ransomed captured guerrillas apparently to perpetuate low-level conflict in drug-producing areas, thereby justifying a continued military presence.[24] According to Luis Zambrano, a former sub-prefect of Tocache, 'the main aim of the Army commander in this area is to maintain the state of emergency ... [SL] operate with impunity, because they know they will always be set free'.[25] Military protection for drug-traffickers appears to have included preventing Peruvian and US anti-drug forces from entering trafficking zones and informing traffickers about forthcoming raids on air-strips and laboratories.[26] Officers stationed in Tocache used counter-insurgency funds to build air-strips north of the town.

Map I *Sudan*

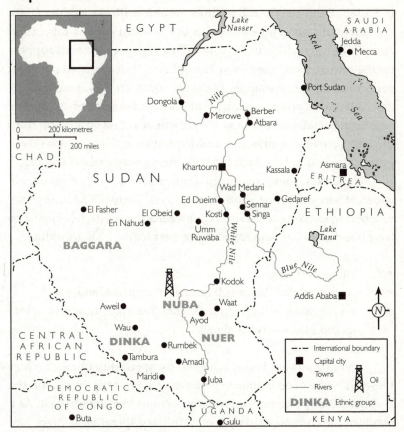

Alienating Civilians

The aggression of counter-insurgency forces has repeatedly alienated their potential civilian supporters, and has often continued
even when evidently counter-productive from a military point of
view. While this has frequently reflected a military ethos that prefers
using massive force to winning hearts and minds, it is not sufficient
to regard this behaviour as simply a mistake.[27] Rebels have tried to
provoke government repression in the hope that official abuse of
civilians will have precisely these counter-productive effects. The
Front pour la Libération Nationale (FLN) used this tactic during the
Algerian war of independence in 1954–62, for example.[28] Rebels too
have sometimes strengthened civilian support for the 'other side'
through their abuses.

The radicalisation of the population through abuse is evident in Sudan. From 1983, Arab militias mounted attacks against *Dinka* civilians with no connection with the Sudan People's Liberation Army (SPLA) rebellion in the south. This violence increased support for the rebels among the *Dinka*. The SPLA in turn alienated potential supporters by encouraging raids on southern Sudanese groups associated with pro-government militias. Mohammed Siyad Barre's regime in Somalia encouraged the growth of armed opposition from the late 1970s by oppressing and exploiting civilians from ethnic groups deemed to be associated with the country's rebel factions.

In Turkey, some 300,000 government troops have been unable to defeat a long-running Kurdistan Workers' Party (PKK) insurgency numbering 4,000–5,000. Several counter-insurgency tactics appear to have boosted, rather than reduced, support for the PKK, including:

- village-burning;
- large-scale forcible displacement of civilians; and
- a system of 'village guards' that has contributed to wide-spread human-rights abuse.

What goals are being achieved by apparent failures such as these? A range of economic benefits may at least partly explain the Turkish military's counter-productive actions in the south-east. As a result of the continued insurgency, military spending is high, and personnel in insecure areas receive substantial bonus payments. Village chiefs, some of whom are involved in drug-trafficking, are paid for organising local guard forces and granted partial immunity from prosecution. The profits from renting and building property in towns housing Kurdish refugees have created a boom economy. Finally, the military's prominent role in politics is partly justified by the continued threat posed by Kurdish terrorism.[29]

These examples illustrate how vested interests both within the military and outside it may inhibit fresh thinking about tactics that appear to be failing to end hostilities. If it is assumed that the only rationale in a conflict is to win it, much of the behaviour from all sides in contemporary civil wars appears bizarre. It begins to make sense only when the desire to stay alive, to make money and, perhaps, to eliminate political, rather than simply military, threats is given proper weight.

chapter 2

'Top-down' Economic Violence

Outside support during the Cold War often helped governments –
and rebel groups – to feed, pay and discipline their security
personnel. Superpowers also tended to overlook the sins of friendly
regimes. While the Soviet bloc backed governments in countries as
diverse as Afghanistan, Angola, Cambodia, Ethiopia, Mozambique
and Nicaragua, the West propped up those in El Salvador,
Guatemala, Kenya, Liberia, Somalia, Sudan and Zaire. Declining
Cold War tensions threatened this support. External funding
declined, limiting the resources that many states could use for
repression, while the tendency to link continued aid with human-
rights observance increased. Even for states such as Rwanda and
Sierra Leone, which had avoided direct superpower alliances, the
end of the Cold War gave new life to calls for democracy, as well as
international pressure for economic prudence.

These developments may have been expected to lead to a
general decline in state violence. This has not, however, been the
case. Instead, states have increasingly resorted to violence that is
effectively self-financing, while stepping up efforts to disguise their
responsibility for human-rights abuse. A common technique has
been to incite ethnic strife by recruiting supporters and fighters
along ethnic lines and sponsoring the formation of ethnic militias.
This conflict, which is easiest to generate in countries with a history
of ethnic violence and where ethnicity cuts across class lines, is then
used to mask or explain human-rights abuse. States have used

ethnic conflict not only to defeat insurgency, but also to delay the advent of democracy and – a related aim – to carve out a sphere of economic and political influence within collapsing, frequently impoverished states, particularly those that lack a plural political culture.[1] In Liberia, Somalia and the former Yugoslavia, this sphere of influence centred on a territory which, although smaller than the original state boundaries, was as large as its creators could achieve.

Inciting top-down violence may, paradoxically, include encouraging violence by apparent opponents. Regimes have used the threat of another's violence to exploit particular groups (under cover of war), maintain their hold on power or suppress political opposition (under cover of fighting rebels). The violence of an opposing force has also been useful in deflecting responsibility for illicit activities. In Guatemala, Mozambique, Peru and Sierra Leone, rebels have been blamed for crimes carried out by the regular armed forces ranging from looting to drug-running.[2] There is evidence that, with Guatemala's role in the cocaine trade growing in the 1990s, the Guatemalan Army has falsely blamed the URNG for its own drug-trafficking activities. Drug profits contributed to a real-estate boom from which many Army officers benefited.

Conditions for Top-down Violence

Economic violence is violence from which short-term profit is made. Its motivation may not necessarily be purely economic. It may be encouraged or tolerated for political reasons, although ultimately it is provoked to defend economic privileges. Seven conditions can encourage top-down economic violence:

- a weak state;
- rebel movements that lack strong external finance or support;
- an undemocratic or 'exclusive' regime under threat;
- economic crisis;
- ethnic divisions that cut across class lines;
- the existence of valuable commodities; and
- prolonged conflict.

Some countries, Sudan for example, have suffered from most or even all of these conditions at once, and have correspondingly experienced high levels of economic violence. However, not all of these conditions have to be present. Moreover, states cannot be divided neatly between the weak and the strong, and different countries can suffer from economic crises of differing depth and duration. The likelihood of economically motivated violence depends upon the degree to which these conditions apply and interact with each other. For example, economic agendas are likely to be particularly prominent when a fragile and undemocratic state tries to suppress discontent arising from its weakness and autocracy, and where rebels lack strong external support.

A Weak State
Although the relative importance of these conditions varies from case to case, state weakness is generally the most significant. A weak state is unable to impose the rule of law or to provide its people with basic services. Economic violence tends to be important in weak states' civil wars because, in the absence of central funding, élites try to 'privatise' conflict by exploiting the civilian economy. They are also likely to try to incite violence for private gain.

Fighting an 'Economical' War
In Angola, Ethiopia, Liberia, Sierra Leone, Somalia and Zaire – and, to some extent, the former Yugoslavia – governments and faction leaders have used underpaid or unpaid fighters who derive at least part of their income from preying on civilians, or from illegal production

conflicts become 'privatised' in weak states

and trade. This has tended to weaken lines of command within military organisations, making it difficult to instil discipline.

Licensing economically motivated violence in this way has a long history. Well into the eighteenth century, before the advent of strong states in Europe, plundering civilians compensated for late, inadequate or non-existent pay. The economic aims of the participants could at times be explicit: during the Hundred Years' War between England and France in the thirteenth and fourteenth centuries, English military commanders signed complex contracts with the royal authorities stipulating 'the advantages of war', including loot, captured lands and castles.[3]

The rise of modern, bureaucratic states in Europe largely put paid to this financing method. Elsewhere, however, strong states have yet to be properly established or, as in Eastern Europe, have been enfeebled with the end of the Cold War. A state's fragility can reflect a weak economy, often based on agriculture and the export of primary products, and the government's limited ability to raise revenues. As a result, officials are badly paid, making them susceptible to corruption, and capital is short, allowing foreign investors to drive a hard bargain, particularly over the distribution of profits from primary industries such as mining.

During counter-insurgency campaigns, officials can tolerate or encourage paramilitaries or ethnic militias in committing crimes. This is a major factor in creating the 'climate of impunity' condemned by organisations such as Amnesty International in its examinations of human-rights abuse in civil wars. Even when groups associated with the government have legally appropriated assets, they have often only been able to do so because of changes in the law. For example, the Barre regime in Somalia changed the law governing access to land in 1975, transferring the ownership of all land to the state, but allowing groups close to the government privileged access to leaseholds.[4] Sudanese ruler General Jaafar Nimeiri altered the constitutional laws covering ownership of oil in 1983 to ensure that profits from the industry went to the north, rather than to the south. In Sierra Leone in 1992, the law was changed to give the military the right to raid private houses.

Where states are weak and lines of command tenuous or non-existent, official 'protection' for civilians threatened by rebels or bandits can be a mixed blessing. As Eric Hobsbawm notes:

> *Where there is no regular or effective machinery for the maintenance of public order – and this is almost by definition the case where banditry flourishes – there is not much point in appealing to the authorities for protection, all the less so as such an appeal will quite likely bring along an expeditionary force of troops, who will lay waste the countryside far more surely than the local bandits.*[5]

Hobsbawm's observation would strike a chord in Sierra Leone. The insurgency there, which began in 1991, was at first dismissed as the work of bandits and external agitators. After initial vacillation, the government responded by rapidly expanding its military from some

Map 2 *Liberia and Sierra Leone*

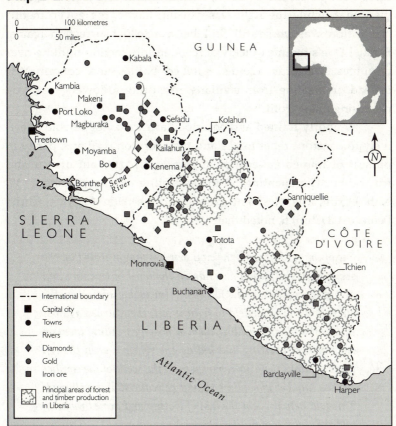

3,000 to around 14,000. It recruited militiamen who had spilled over from the conflict in neighbouring Liberia, as well as local boys who had become separated or estranged from their families. These youths, who were paid virtually nothing, were seen in some quarters as braver than their adult colleagues because they often, at least initially, viewed violence as a 'game'.[6]

    This rag-tag force, under-trained, underpaid and under-fed, was sent into battle against rebels in the fertile and diamond-rich south and east of the country. Government soldiers resorted to raiding and to illegal mining to supplement their inadequate incomes. Zainab Bangura, a prominent Sierra Leonean human-rights campaigner, commented on the new breed of soldiers in June 1995: 'They were drop-outs and robbers. You've legalised their trade'.[7] As the conflict wore on, civilians increasingly expressed the view that, while the RUF was causing havoc, the government's 'protection' was worse still.[8] In Liberia, a 1989 insurrection against Samuel Doe's regime quickly descended into faction-fighting over resources. Warlords avoided pitched battles and concentrated instead on stealing from civilians, recruiting followers partly by promising them profit.

A poorly trained and equipped army may be unable effectively to confront rebel forces and may turn on civilians, partly in pursuit of immediate economic gain and partly out of fear and frustration.[9] Commenting on the escalating conflict in Liberia, W. Nah Dixon, the Resident Bishop of the Don Stewart Christ Pentecostal Church, noted that:

> *one of the great lessons the civil war has taught us is that the security of the nation depends on the level of training and discipline of its armed forces ... Incapable of facing the enemy on the battlefield to fight it out, they turned against innocent civilians, holding them as hostages, killing them on suspicion of abetting and hiding the rebels – even though these civilians were far removed from the scene of the conflict ... The number of soldiers should be reduced and well paid. This will help prevent the lust of looting and armed robbery, and the staging of military coups.*[10]

In 1996 and 1997, the underpaid Zairean Army seemed more interested in looting from civilians than in fighting Laurent Kabila's rebel Alliance of Democratic Forces for the Liberation of Congo-Zaire (ADFL). Although not new in Zaire, such acquisitive behaviour appeared especially marked during what was an outright rebellion.[11] In Mozambique, as in Sierra Leone, attacks purportedly by rebels took place suspiciously close to Army checkpoints; large companies like British Petroleum (BP) found themselves obliged to buy off corrupt members of Mozambique's *Frente para a Libertação de Moçambique* (Frelimo) government to avoid 'Renamo' attacks.[12] Even overtly 'religious' conflicts have assumed important economic dimensions. The Khartoum regime has manipulated ethnic violence to reduce the costs of its conflict with the SPLA. In Algeria, the government's arming of 'civil-defence' militias against Islamist insurgents has apparently encouraged economic violence, particularly highway robbery.[13]

Rewarding Cooperation and Deflecting Discontent

Provoking economic violence makes possible not only defraying the costs of waging war, but also rewarding supporters and reducing the discontent of groups which might otherwise join rebel factions. In the 1970s, a series of coup attempts spearheaded by the *Ansar* religious organisation threatened to topple Sudan's military regime under Nimeiri. In response, the regime tried to appease the principal supporters of the *Ansar*, the deprived *Baggara* of western Sudan, by sanctioning their raiding and exploitation of the *Dinka* and *Nuer* in the south. Successive governments have continued this policy, sometimes with slight variations. The civilian coalition government of 1986–89 was accused by elements of the Army of trying to weaken the military by embroiling it in a war of attrition against the SPLA in the south while attempting to build an alternative power-base through *Baggara* militias. In Somalia, the Barre regime's approval of its supporters' dispossession of small farmers in the Jubba and Shabeelle River areas in the 1980s is part of a similar process.[14]

Sanctioning violence in this way has historical precedents. Under colonial regimes in Sudan and elsewhere, political stability depended on 'divide and rule' tactics and implicit agreements between imperial rulers and local élites.[15] In return for remitting a portion of their revenues to central government and keeping the peace in their areas, these élites were allowed to accumulate wealth on their own account. Colonial policy involved official tolerance of violence against particular groups, particularly those seen to be resisting colonial rule. In Sudan, the British encouraged *Baggara* raids against the rebellious *Dinka*.

Warfare has also been used to keep unruly fighters or ethnic groups occupied and rewarded. The suppression of revolt in Ireland in the mid-seventeenth century was a convenient way of occupying disgruntled English troops refusing to disband after the Civil War.[16] The Ottoman Empire armed Kurdish militias during the late nineteenth century and granted them a 'licence to raid' in what appears to have been an effort to appease the Kurds and suppress dissenting Armenians.[17] Finally, the threat of disorder by unemployed or under-employed urban youths has encouraged governments in

Liberia and Sierra Leone to recruit them for military operations. Potentially restive refugees in Sierra Leone and Somalia have also been enlisted.

Warlords, Mercenaries and Mafiosi

Other élite actors looking to improve their economic and political position can also foment top-down violence in weak states. Stephen Ellis argues that radical political and economic reform in Africa in the 1980s and 1990s has unwittingly created the optimum conditions for this:

> *Politicians have lost their ability to secure political acquiescence by the distribution of patronage through the organs of government. Instead, political rivals have taken to building power-bases through informal means, especially the use of private armies and the control of international trade.*[18]

Liberian rebel leader Charles Taylor was particularly adept at using contacts he made with foreign companies as a senior procurement official in Doe's government in the early 1990s. These links allowed him to establish lucrative export trades in iron ore, timber and agricultural products from territory he seized as a warlord. Taylor used these exports, in turn, to boost his military power; the French, fearful of Nigeria's growing influence in Liberia, were particularly keen customers.[19] Taylor enjoyed important financial backing from remnants of the US–Liberian élite, ousted by Doe in 1980, which saw the civil war as an opportunity to re-establish their influence.[20]

Declining foreign aid has encouraged élites to use more violent methods of making money and building political support. This appears to have been particularly important in the disintegration of Liberia and Somalia, both of which were, in the 1980s, dominated by Western-backed autocrats. In Angola, gaining control of diamond wealth under the cover of war has created large private fortunes for the UNITA leadership. The clashes that followed the November 1994 Lusaka peace accords were particularly serious in the diamond district of Lunda Norte, where government forces fought against both UNITA and illegal diamond-miners. *Movimento Popular de Libertação de Angola* (MPLA) provincial leaders used state repression to defend their corruption and exploitation of wartime shortages. The military leadership of both the MPLA and UNITA opposed post-Lusaka demobilisation as undermining their status and position.[21]

If elections are impending, warlords may be able to benefit by promising peace, and through their ability to command a substantial electoral following in their areas of influence. Those who are most violent may, paradoxically, make the most convincing claim that a vote for them is a vote for peace. This has helped even reviled warlords such as UNITA's Jonas Savimbi, Renamo leader Afonso Dhlakama and Taylor. Again, these developments are variations on a much older theme. As Hobsbawm observes, pre-capitalist landowners often tried to harness the power of bandits, since these could be:

> *a local reservoir of uncommitted armed men who, if they can be induced to accept the patronage of some gentleman or magnate, will greatly add to his prestige and may well on a suitable occasion add to his fighting or vote-getting force.*[22]

In weak states, economically motivated violence in civil wars seems to be linked with peacetime corruption. The frailty of Sierra Leone's counter-insurgency appears to reflect the involvement of soldiers and policemen in peacetime smuggling, notably of diamonds. Just as poorly paid and badly trained soldiers may be unable or unwilling to confront rebels in resource-rich areas of Cambodia or Sierra Leone, so too are police officers reluctant to face criminals in Moscow or Warsaw, particularly if the criminals are involved in lucrative illicit trades such as drugs and prostitution.

privatising violence in weak states

In Latin America and Russia and elsewhere in the former Eastern bloc, the post-Cold War decline of external threats, an increasing emphasis on free markets and reduced government spending have cut defence budgets. Since this has usually not coincided with commensurate reductions in armed forces, pay cuts have been widespread and soldiers have turned to a second job, or to corruption. Russian security personnel have 'defected' to the criminal world.[23] Black-market sales of Russian weapons to criminals and insurgents, for example in Chechnya, have combined with the fragmentation of the military to pose a more immediate security threat than any notional Russian military aggression.[24] Declining external threats have also made the military in many Asian countries reassess its role. Armed forces may decide that maintaining internal threats may offer a way of sustaining current levels of military spending.

A state unable to protect its citizens' property may compel its people to hire fighters to do so. Writing on the role of criminal mafias in Sicily and Russia, Federico Varese suggests that 'privatising' protection tends to become more common when state weakness coincides with a readily available pool of suitably qualified, unemployed fighters. In late nineteenth century Sicily, redundant soldiers and the former guards of dwindling feudal estates filled this role. Unemployed or demoralised security personnel are abundant in the former Soviet Union.[25] The 'demobilised' security apparatus of South Africa's apartheid regime has provided the main source of recruits for private military companies like Executive Outcomes (EO).[26] EO played a positive role in facilitating elections in Sierra Leone in 1996.[27] However, commercial considerations may encourage these companies to neglect areas that are not rich in resources. These companies may also make arrangements with multinationals that exclude locals, thereby fuelling resentment and, in the longer term, conflict.

The expansion of the private military sector should be seen in the context of the growth of private security more generally. The increase in the number of civil-defence organisations is another sign of the importance of economic agendas in civil wars. It also illustrates the weak political will in some countries behind official counter-insurgency or crime-fighting initiatives. From 1993, civilians in Sierra Leone, faced with the twin threat of attacks by rebel and government soldiers, provided funding and personnel for nascent civil-defence groups. Although poorly armed, these bands sometimes intimidated undisciplined gunmen, including government soldiers, into tempering their activities. They also helped to establish the conditions in which elections became possible in 1996. In warlord-ravaged Somalia, Islamic courts became increasingly influential in the early 1990s, and challenged faction leader Mohammed Farah Aideed by setting up an alternative justice system, based on *Shari'a* law, in south Mogadishu. Vigilantes have also been paid to protect particular neighbourhoods.[28] Civil-defence groups are not confined to states with civil wars: vigilante groups have been formed in South Africa in response to escalating crime and the inadequate performance of poorly paid government security forces. Criminal and vigilante groups appear to provide a role for under-employed young men half-trained by the African National Congress (ANC) when in opposition.

Economic agendas may be actively taken up by self-defence organisations. Sierra Leone's inadequately paid civil-defence recruits have become involved in diamond-mining, often clashing with government soldiers for mining rights. In Colombia, where the Army and police have been largely unable to protect civilians from guerrillas, *declining external support encourages internal plunder* self-defence organisations have waged a significantly more effective campaign. The drug-traffickers who funded these paramilitary groups did so to defend the estates into which they had invested much of their drug profits.[29] These groups also became tools of political repression. In 1989, then Colombian President Virgilio Barco admitted that:

> *Criminal actions are shielded in vain behind anti-Communism and the struggle against the guerrillas. In reality, the majority of [the paramilitaries'] victims are not guerrillas. They are men, women and even children, who have not taken up arms against institutions.*[30]

Rebels with Weak External Support

Rebels may exploit civilians to fight a war; they may also fight a war to exploit civilians. Ideologically committed rebel leaders – Mao Zedong, Che Guevara and Ho Chi Minh – banned economic violence among their forces, and produced highly disciplined movements as a result. In contrast to counter-insurgency forces, which tended to comprise troops from foreign countries, rebel leaderships often emerged from the civilian population. This frequently fostered a more benevolent attitude towards civilians: while rebels at times alienated the civilians on which they relied, such politically suicidal behaviour has historically been rare.[31]

This seems to be changing as Cold War external support for rebel movements declines and revolutionary political ideologies disintegrate.[32] While governments have recourse to taxation and other legal means to fund a war effort, rebels have to rely on external finance, 'gifts' or theft. They have therefore tended to increase their efforts to accumulate funds from domestic sources – either for military purposes or for private gain. UNITA, the Khmer Rouge and elements of the opposition under opium warlord Khun Sa in Myanmar have all gravitated from a strong ideological agenda to one dominated by economic aims. Apparently 'mindless' rebel violence often makes sense in this context. Rebels lacking substantial resources may resort to brutality in a bid to create maximum impact with minimum funding, and to depopulate resource-rich areas.[33]

In southern Africa, the erosion of Cold War divisions has combined with the end of apartheid in South Africa to weaken external backing for UNITA and Renamo. Renamo's increased pillaging in the late 1980s was related to its loss of direct South African support in the wake of the 'Nkomati Accord on Non-Aggression and Good Neighbourliness' between Pretoria and Maputo in 1984.[34] UNITA has increasingly relied on the revenues from diamonds smuggled through the DROC.[35]

The RUF in Sierra Leone was not in a position to benefit from Cold War rivalries since its insurgency began only in 1991. It therefore concentrated at an early stage on taking control of the country's diamond mines. What external support the group did attract came from Taylor, who was more interested in gaining access to diamonds than in inspiring and funding an ideological revolution.

Economic agendas have become increasingly prominent among Colombia's insurgent groups. Guerrillas maintained a strong presence in the rebel stronghold of Middle Magdalene Valley from the early 1960s. Initially, demands for funds were limited to large landowners but, as these fled the area, guerrillas increasingly targeted smaller farmers, undermining their political support-base.[36] Although the inequalities that initially prompted rebellion persist, the drive to overthrow the government has been succeeded by demands for agrarian reform and licence to operate freely within areas of influence.[37] As ideology fades, some guerrillas have integrated into the political system, or have simply turned to outright crime.[38] The *Fuerzas Armadas Revolucionarias de Colombia* (FARC), once a firmly Marxist–Leninist group, is now known as the 'third cartel', after those in Medellín and Cali, because of its deep involvement in the drugs trade.[39] FARC has levied taxes at each stage of the growing, processing and shipment process; in 1992, the coca and opium trades accounted for an estimated 70% of its revenue. Kidnapping was its second-highest earner, followed by extortion and gold-mining.[40]

The emergence of rebel economic agendas has prompted 'rebellions within rebellions', as the aims of sections of an insurgent group diverge or resources within the group are unevenly distributed. By late 1990, Taylor was becoming unpopular with many of his original supporters among the *Gio* and *Mano* ethnic groups, who increasingly saw him as 'a business executive waging a corporate take-over war on Liberia'.[41] Renamo's plundering was both an insurance against unreliable foreign support and a source of resentment and mutiny among its soldiers.[42] The SPLA was deprived of Ethiopian backing with the fall of the dictator Mengistu Haile Mariam in 1991, encouraging increasing economic violence among southern Sudanese factions.

International assistance for cross-border refugees – Cambodians in Thailand, Ethiopians in Somalia and Afghans in Pakistan, for example – has been an important source of support for rebel movements. Providing humanitarian help has been a convenient and seemingly 'apolitical' way for international actors to support rebel movements, typically those fighting a Cold War struggle.[43] The new tendency to focus on helping refugees in their country of origin seems to have combined with diminishing Cold War tensions to limit this form of backing.[44] This has had serious consequences for the finances of a number of rebel movements, among them the Khmer Rouge in Cambodia and Thailand and the SPLA in Sudan and Ethiopia.

Undemocratic Regimes under Threat
Regimes that are undemocratic, exclude significant groups from government and face a rebel threat have incited violence to maintain

their grip on power. Independence from colonial rule rarely ushered in democracy. Post-colonial governments tended to be dominated by

undemocratic regimes in weak states have fuelled economic violence

the same élites, often from specific ethnic groups or geographical areas, that had wielded influence under colonial regimes. This was particularly the case in states where there was little nationalist mass-mobilisation to force independence, such as Sierra Leone and Sudan.

These élites continued to benefit at the expense of the majority from post-colonial development. At the same time, unrepresentative regimes – those of Doe in Liberia, Barre in Somalia and Juvénal Habyarimana in Rwanda, for example – were buttressed by foreign aid prompted by the Cold War and other geopolitical rivalries, such as that between the British and French in Rwanda.[45]

The end of the Cold War, by boosting pro-democracy movements and reducing outside support for abusive regimes, has increased the pressure on unrepresentative governments, making them more likely to resort to violence. From the former Yugoslavia to Rwanda and Sudan, moves towards democracy have helped to trigger large-scale violence, rather than smooth the way to peace and government by consent. In Rwanda, élites from the *Akazu* branch of the *Hutu* were prepared to incite genocide rather than allow the advent of democratic government or *Hutu–Tutsi* cooperation within the political opposition.[46]

Rwanda is a small country with a traditionally strong state apparatus. The genocide unleashed there was carefully orchestrated; killing, rather than looting, was its main objective, although plundering became more common as the genocide proceeded. Encouraging more specifically economic violence has been particularly marked where undemocratic regimes have ruled over weak states. This violence has often been caused by stoking ethnic tensions. Ethnic politics can be the simplest way of recruiting supporters and undermining those keen to organise a class struggle. Undemocratic regimes have repeatedly disavowed ethnic politics even as they manipulated it from behind the scenes. Barre dramatised his 'burial' of ethnic politics by ordering the symbolic burial of coffins in Somali towns. Yet his regime, like those of former Zairean President Mobutu Sese Seko, Doe and Iraq's Saddam

Hussein, sought to build political support among particular families, clans and ethnic groups by granting them economic privileges, including the right to inflict violence on others.

In Sudan, ethnic groups seen as threatening or rebellious, particularly those in the south, have not only been dispossessed of land and cattle but also exploited through markets skewed against them by force. In the early 1980s, the discovery of oil in the south, the increasing influence of Islamic fundamentalists in the north and the growth of democratic forces throughout the country encouraged Khartoum to divide the opposition. From 1983, the regime incited attacks on the south which, in 1986–89, became a major economic war. A variety of factors, including the difficulty of holding elections in the war-torn south and racial discrimination in ministerial appointments, meant that southerners lacked significant representation in Khartoum. This political exclusion not only fuelled discontent, but also deprived southerners and the *Nuba*, who live at the southern extreme of the north, of redress against state repression. Political exclusion deepened as exploitation prompted increased resistance and further opportunities for stigmatising those associated with the rebellion.

Although conflict with opposition forces may threaten undemocratic regimes, it can also have its uses. It provides an opportunity to reward supporters, and can help to legitimise authoritarian or military rule. Conflict may be used to stifle political opposition by declaring and prolonging states of emergency that grant special powers to repressive governments or to the military, and through restrictions on freedom of speech justified as part of a 'war effort'. Kenyan President Daniel arap Moi has used the threat of ethnic conflict to justify one-party politics, while at the same time fomenting ethnic tensions.[47] Prolonging conflict may also make elections impracticable. This appears to have been one of the aims of attacks against Sierra Leonean civilians by government troops posing as rebels in 1994–95. Preventing elections from taking place may be particularly important for those who, under a more democratic regime, may face prosecution for violence or exploitation.

During the Vietnam War, the Saigon regime used measures ostensibly aimed at the Viet Cong to suppress other opposition. As Charles Maechling notes:

> *Although supposedly targeted exclusively against NLF*
> *[National Liberation Front or Viet Cong] stalwarts, the*
> *Phoenix program [which was supposed to eliminate the Viet*
> *Cong political apparatus in the villages through*
> *assassination] was largely used by the Saigon regime to*
> *liquidate the non-Communist political opposition and NLF*
> *'sympathisers' – an effort that further alienated the mass of*
> *civilians.*[48]

The concept of 'rebel' may be kept conveniently fluid. Speaking just before his assassination in 1989, Ramon Emilio Arcila, leader of Colombia's 'civic movement' in Eastern Antioquia, said:

> *leaders from all the regions of Colombia have been*
> *assassinated. They are indiscriminately linked with the*
> *armed movements to justify the repression. The state has*
> *issued a series of repressive measures in which any*
> *expression or demonstration practically constitutes a*
> *terrorist act, and leads to searches and arrests.*[49]

In the 1990s, the Western-backed regime in Algeria has repeatedly blamed massacres on Islamic extremists, a view that the Western media was content to accept. By 1997, however, it had become clear that members of the regime had actively encouraged the climate of insecurity in the country apparently to perpetuate military rule.[50] Western intelligence services believe that the security forces have infiltrated the extremist *Groupe Islamique Armée* (GIA), and are deeply implicated in the cycle of killings.[51] The government has opposed setting up an international commission of inquiry into the massacres.

Economic Crisis
Economic crisis can increase top-down violence; violence in turn can increase economic crisis. The cost of conflict may weaken a state's ability to protect its people through an efficient legal system and police force. This can encourage crime and organised banditry, prompting people to turn to private militias or warlords for security. Economic difficulties relate to top-down violence in three main ways:

- encouraging ethnic or religious tensions to deflect attention away from the economy;
- making more urgent the need to secure resources through violence; and
- creating the conditions for insurgency while reducing the resources available to suppress it.

Encouraging ethnic or religious tensions to defuse economic discontent appears most likely in states where these hostilities are already strongly present, and where a crisis poses a political threat to business interests. German conservatives and businessmen combined in the 1930s to assist Hitler's rise to power in the belief that the Nazi Party offered a favourable alternative to the communists as an outlet for popular frustration at the state of the economy. Government-sponsored ethnic conflict in Sudan can be seen as an attempt to prevent the SPLA from uniting economically marginalised groups in the north with those in the south.

Economic crisis seems to make more urgent the need to secure resources by violent means. Dwindling aid inflows increased pillaging in Somalia in the late 1980s. In Liberia and Sierra Leone, falling prices and revenues for key export commodities in the 1980s contributed to the transition from a corrupt state administration to a pattern of economically motivated violence in which state officials were implicated. The heavily indebted Sudanese government used northern militia to attack the southern *Dinka* in an effort to gain access to oil resources in the south. These reserves were Khartoum's only way of repaying its escalating international debt. The Arab militia-members, themselves facing economic difficulties as mechanised farms expanded into their traditional grazing areas, benefited from their exploitation of the south. The *Dinka*, by contrast, suffered a devastating famine as their economy was undermined.

Economic crisis can create the conditions in which an insurgency flourishes, while reducing a government's capacity to tackle it. In the 1980s, the Sierra Leonean government's ability to provide essential social services was hampered by a combination of falling export revenues, austerity programmes and the growth of private monopolies that drew finance from the Treasury. This helped to prompt rebellion in areas of the south and east that had come close to being abandoned by the state.

Ethnic Divisions

Private economic violence is less likely in rebellions underwritten by a coherent ideology and a strong sense of class than in those that are not. A variety of ideologically driven rebel leaders have encouraged self-discipline among their

politics has often been overlaid with short-term economic aims

forces to maintain civilian support. Political or ideological struggles have also been more prominent than economic violence when class divides have coincided with ethnic divisions, for example in states where large areas of land have been seized by foreigners and indigenous people have been pushed aside. Conflicts in Latin America have been strongly influenced by these processes, as have many anti-colonial wars. However, even in these circumstances, politics has often been overlaid with short-term economic aims. Ethnic divisions within an insurgency are likely to erode ideological coherence, as in South Africa, while economic agendas have sometimes become increasingly important over time, as in Colombia.

In the absence of a colonial power or a major land seizure, it may be difficult for rebels to preserve the political character of their movement. This is partly why post-colonial and African wars have tended to be more 'economic' than anti-colonial and non-African ones. When a sense of class or nationalism is weakly developed, it may be easier to recruit people into ethnic violence, perhaps stemming initially from a top-down initiative designed to turn one disgruntled group against another.

The strength of the SPLA in southern Sudan reflects the regime's discrimination against non-Arab groups through development initiatives that concentrated wealth in the centre and east of the country. However, the SPLA's attempts to recruit a broad-based class constituency comprising all those neglected by the regime have been undermined by alliances between privileged Arab interests in Khartoum and under-privileged Arab herders in western Sudan.

Resources and Trade

Economic violence will be more likely when the potential rewards are great. Valuable natural resources and trading opportunities arising from conflict can both increase the economic benefits of war. When the resources actually commanded by either a regime or a rebel leadership are small compared with those potentially available in areas of conflict, economically motivated violence is particularly likely.

Rebellions have often been concentrated in resource-rich areas. This is partly because local people feel that they have not benefited from the resources in their area, and partly because these regions can sustain rebel movements. In Sierra Leone, diamond-rich areas in the east have been a consistent focus of rebel activity. In Colombia, rebels have gradually shifted towards territory relatively rich in oil and drugs. In Somalia in the 1990s, conflict has been concentrated in the resource-rich lower Jubba, lower Shabeelle and Mogadishu areas; violence has often been between non-indigenous clans.[52]

Government forces sent to resource-rich areas may be distracted from suppressing a rebellion, particularly if they are underpaid. It can be argued that many of the guerrilla movements that have taken power in Africa – in Chad, Ethiopia and Uganda, for example – were spurred on by the relative lack of valuable local resources. More abundant resources may have diverted them into more directly economic violence such as that in Angola and Sierra Leone. The lack of valuable resources in Renamo-held areas of Mozambique may have been a factor in reconciling its leaders to peace in December 1992. In Cambodia and Liberia, military stalemate seems to have encouraged economic accumulation by rebel groups unable to seize control of the capital city.

Economic violence among rebels is more likely when natural resources can be exploited with minimal technology and without the need to control the capital or machinery of the state. The value of resources depends on the demand for them, and trade routes and networks to export them. Precious stones, especially those that can be mined with relatively simple technology, are a common source of finance. Diamonds have helped to provoke and sustain economic violence in Angola, Liberia and Sierra Leone. The Khmer Rouge has made large profits from the gem trade on the Thai–Cambodian border. The timber trade has also been important for the Khmer Rouge, as well as for government officials and the military. Timber was critical in sustaining Taylor's 'empire' in Liberia. Again, this does not require particularly complex technology.

Drug-growing, apparently encouraged by the US, was vital to the Afghan *mujaheddin* during their war with the Soviet Union in the

1980s. Drugs have played an important part in supporting insurgency in Colombia, and were central to SL's finances. In the late 1980s, the group earned $20–30 million a year from taxing cocaine processing and shipping in the Upper Huallaga Valley. Some Peruvian dealers paid SL for exclusive rights to operate in a particular territory or for guerrilla 'protection' against rivals.[53] The *Movimiento Revolucionario Túpac*

even bandits need to sell what they steal

Amaru (MRTA), whose hostage-seizure at the Japanese embassy in Lima in 1996 attracted world-wide attention, has also drawn vital finance from drug operations in the Upper Huallaga Valley.

Exporting commodities such as oil may require greater organisation and investment. In Angola, Savimbi has appeared unable to choose between local influence over diamond production and a position in Luanda, where oil revenues are controlled and allocated. Oil has fuelled secessionist movements in Biafra, Sudan and Angola's Cabinda enclave. Colombia's *Ejército de Liberación Nacional* (ELN) rebel group concentrates on attacking the oil and gas infrastructure.[54] Its revival since the mid-1980s has been linked with protection payments from German companies involved in oil production and pipeline construction.[55] Competition for scarce agricultural resources such as grazing land can also be a source of economic violence, both by rebels and by government forces.

Investment and trade are important, even for outlaws: Hobsbawm points out that even bandits need to sell what they steal. They therefore need to work with traders; for finance, they may need money-lenders. They also need information, for example the schedules and routes of convoys they may wish to intercept. These links help to explain how 'rural toughs' in Corsica and Sicily could 'transform themselves into Mafiosi businessmen' dealing in drugs and luxury hotels.[56]

Price changes caused by civil wars may open trading opportunities by affecting the availability of commodities – by creating a food emergency or by compelling people to sell assets, for example. The profits from unusual price movements help to explain why economic agendas tend to become more pronounced as a civil war develops. Violence may create or maintain trading monopolies:

soldiers may, for example, threaten civilian traders; rival factions may vie for control of trade in particular areas.

Both international sanctions and emergency aid during conflict can increase the opportunities for profitable dealing and may act as a further incentive to use violence to control trade. Frequently, the political élites targeted by international sanctions (for example, in Serbia and Iraq) are best placed to profit from them.[57] More selective sanctions may be one answer to this problem.

Prolonged Conflict

The longer a civil war, the more likely it becomes that people will find ways to profit from it.[58] It also becomes more likely that fighting will intensify as resources diminish. This may lead to conflict within a rebel movement, such as that between Kurdish factions in northern Iraq from 1993 as embargoes from both the UN and Baghdad reignited old schisms. Governments in war-torn countries have typically faced a drop in tax revenue as conflict sends the formal economy into sharp decline. The resources commanded by the state have tended to fall significantly from a base that may already be low. When a long-running civil war has caused massive economic damage, a regime's survival may depend on its ability to exploit the 'war economy' to build political support.

Combining Conditions

Where several of the conditions described in this chapter apply at once, economic violence is particularly probable. Top-down violence is especially likely when an undemocratic regime faces a substantial political or military threat, and where the weakness of the state means that central funding is not available to fight a counter-insurgency. Under these circumstances, regimes tend to respond by provoking economic violence, often along ethnic lines. In countries with valuable local resources such as Angola, Cambodia, Liberia and Sierra Leone, or with lucrative drug-trafficking industries such as Afghanistan and Peru, government forces will be tempted to accumulate short-term, local profits. Where a rebel movement lacks adequate external finance, its soldiers may find themselves in a position similar to that of troops working for a weak state. They are not being paid, and so need to raise resources locally, usually through violent means. This can easily degenerate into making profits for its own sake, rather than to fund a political struggle.

The longer a war lasts, the more likely economically motivated violence appears to be. Although some insurgent groups may have sufficient commitment to maintain a political struggle, the decline of communism seems to have diluted the ideological content of many rebellions. However, although the end of the Cold War has been welcomed as a victory for capitalism, free markets need not imply peace. Free enterprise can easily dovetail into economic violence, and self-help into helping oneself.

chapter 3

'Bottom-up' Economic Violence

Many ordinary people participate in violence because they are forced to do so, but some may deliberately *embrace* it for specific, short-term purposes. The line between coercion and voluntary recruitment may be difficult to draw, particularly when attacks on civilians are widespread. It may, for example, be more dangerous to stay out of an armed band than to join one. In Liberia and Sierra Leone, unarmed and unaffiliated young men have been particularly vulnerable to accusations of collaboration with either government or rebel forces.

The spread of powerful, cheap light weapons makes it particularly important to understand bottom-up violence. As societies become better armed, warfare is more likely to involve an arrangement between élites and the civilians they wish to recruit. Violence will increasingly serve a purpose for those at the bottom of a society, as well as for those at the top. When a state tries to harness social tensions to prompt conflict, the nature of the resulting violence will reflect the priorities of social groups, as well as of the state. All civil wars reflect shifting coalitions between military organisations and the civilian population.

When ordinary people actively embrace violence, they may be seeking revolutionary political change or venting ethnic hatred. They may also be trying to meet other, more immediate or mundane needs. Rather than portraying bottom-up violence as 'political' or, where this label does not apply, 'irrational', it may be more useful to investigate some of its more short-term uses. The violent may be intent on preserving their physical security; they may be looking for excitement or for the immediate rectification of a perceived wrong. They may also be following their own *economic* agendas. Even apparently mindless acts of violence can make sense in this context.

Conditions for Bottom-up Violence

Some of the factors that encourage top-down economic violence can also encourage it from the bottom up. When, for example, a weak state cannot guarantee its citizens' economic or physical security, ordinary people appear particularly prone to turn to violence. Prolonged conflict can also prompt bottom-up, as well as top-down, violence. For the majority, continued fighting deepens poverty and damages agriculture and industry. Economic disruption during a war may encourage young men in particular to turn to military options for an income. Prolonged conflict is also likely to reduce the resources available to the state and to encourage it to spend what remains on security, rather than on social services. As war is turned against civilians, they may themselves be forced to resort to violence. These shared conditions aside, three factors are particularly conducive to generating bottom-up violence:

- deep social and economic exclusion;
- the absence of a strong revolutionary organisation; and
- impunity for violent acts.

Social and Economic Exclusion

Violence may meet an individual's basic needs when long-term under-development and economic and social exclusion mean that peaceful behaviour does not. Marginalised sections of the population have for centuries turned to organised banditry. In twelfth and thirteenth century France, disadvantaged regions provided a high proportion of the mercenaries breaking away from the King's control and refusing to disband.[1] These areas were

> regions of poor soils, uplands or lands where men were already feeling too constricted, but also regions on the periphery of the kingdom of France. The sources agree in seeing the routiers [brigands] both as poor men, even

uprooted by their miserable condition, and as men excluded
from the normal ranks of society.[2]

The Crusades held a particular attraction for landless younger sons whose prospects of inheritance were poor. Popes played openly on the potential for enrichment in their appeals for assistance.[3]

Mark Chingono suggests that the role of young men in violence cannot be properly understood without looking at economic factors such as unemployment.[4] In Sierra Leone, a chronic shortage of employment opportunities has been matched by a contraction in educational ones, causing many youths to rebel in search of wealth and status. Young militiamen in Liberia, suffering from

even genocide can have an economic purpose

a similar lack of opportunity, have based themselves in areas rich in diamonds or crops, or where humanitarian convoys could be looted. Thieving from civilians and commandeering slave labour have been commonplace. In Rwanda, the opportunity to ease chronic land-shortages may have encouraged ordinary *Hutus* to participate in the 1994 genocide.

Guerrillas in Latin America have used government anti-drug initiatives to gain the support of the coca-growing peasants affected. In Peru, guerrillas have provided political 'guidance' and armed protection for peasants faced with government drug-eradication programmes and exploitation by drug dealers. Vigorous interception of drug flights from Peru to Colombia had, by late 1995, caused a drastic fall in coca-leaf and paste prices as traders became less eager for the product. This prompted an emergency feeding programme by USAID. SL exploited the crisis to regain support in the Upper Huallaga Valley.[5] FARC and ELN

> *administer vast coca cultivation zones in several Colombian*
> *departments ... Guerrillas act as a kind of surrogate*
> *government in these zones; the protective function extends to*
> *supporting (or organizing) episodes of peasant resistance*
> *against the Colombian government's anti-coca policies.*[6]

Even violence that initially appears purposeless can make sense if social and economic exclusion is taken into account. In both Liberia and Rwanda, genocide seems to have offered opportunities not only for looting, but also for venting fury against those perceived as enjoying unfair economic advantages. Far from being random or meaningless, abuse by both government and RUF forces in Sierra Leone can be explained as reflecting the deep resentment of young men denied a substantial role or status within their communities. Teenage fighters repeatedly humiliated chiefs and local 'big men'. Violence such as this may have aimed to heal what Nigerian writer Femi Osofisan has called the 'wound of invisibility'. Hobsbawm argues that killing and torture 'is the most primitive and personal assertion of ultimate power, and the weaker the rebel feels himself to be at bottom, the greater, we may suppose, the temptation to assert it'.[7] In Sierra Leone – an avid consumer of Western products – status and power could be expressed in terms of Western role models. According to an aid worker with the Council of Churches of Sierra Leone:

> *Before the war, there was a run-down of the system. A lot of the youths had dropped out of the school system, or were still in but not very interested ... By fighting, you get a lot of money and excitement and see the country. You're going from being nothing in a village to being Rambo.*[8]

One local worker with Catholic Relief Services spelt out the link between poor educational facilities and rebellion in 1995:

> *The educational system has increased rebel and soldier numbers. A lot drop out of school early, and these do not have fair job opportunities. And having gone to school, they do not want to go back to their villages and till the land. They feel they are a little too enlightened to go back and till the soil! They feel their friends will laugh at them, and say you are still farming even though you went off to school. They saw that being a rebel you can loot at will, then you have a sway over your former master, who used to lord it over you, or the others who might have laughed. You might as well go to the bush and become a rebel. There is no master there.*[9]

This account is particularly illuminating in view of the widespread humiliation by rebels of the civilians they claimed to be liberating.

The humiliation was often compounded by forcing bystanders to laugh or applaud. In Mozambique,

> *disenchanted social strata – the young in particular, who have been unable to obtain secondary school education or upward mobility in the social structure because it has fallen into the hands of the dominant lineage's elders – probably find life with Renamo offering the only alternative, providing some excitement and the potential of authority denied them in their villages, albeit by the barrel of a gun.*[10]

This use of violence to provide a sense of 'worth' in a society that offered minimal respect or opportunity is echoed in anti-colonial struggles. In his analysis of the Algerian war of independence, Robert Malley observes that figures once part of the criminal underworld could be rehabilitated as political heroes.[11] Paul Schulte notes that the 1965 film *The Battle of Algiers* 'shows

violence may provide an immediate sense of power

the FLN offering an alternative "moral career structure" for the disadvantaged' and describes the 'politicised disruption of ordinary life' that makes 'the addictive pleasures of righteous bullying available even to the very young'.[12] For Frantz Fanon, 'at the level of individuals, violence is a cleansing force. It frees the native from his inferiority complex and from his despair and inaction, it makes him fearless and restores his self-respect'.[13]

Even vandalism and apparently aimless destruction may reflect a kind of perverse economic agenda. Hobsbawm notes the special status of a category of bandits he calls 'the avengers': 'Often most admired by those who are most powerless, these "avengers" could embody "a revolution of destruction", which tumbles the whole world in ruins since no "good" world seems possible'. There can, observes Hobsbawm, be social justice in the destruction of wealth.[14] On Sierra Leone, Paul Richards hints at the perverse satisfaction felt by rebels when he observes:

> *In pursuit of a populist vision of political accountability the rebels ... have reduced a country they presumed rotten to the core to ruins. Through their actions the country has become*

> *in reality the wasteland they always supposed it to be ... like*
> *Montana survivors, the rebels find the metropolitan world*
> *corrupted beyond redemption.*[15]

After an attack on the Sierra Rutile mine at Gbangbatok, Sierra
Leone, in January 1995, a former employee pointed out that a senior
staff-member's monthly salary would pay a junior employee for
three years. He added: 'Some people were angry with Rutile, saying
the country's not benefiting and Rutile has spoilt the area, taken land
from people ... Most workers were happy when the attack took
place. They said perhaps that will be a lesson to the Rutile staff –
now we are all in the bush [emphasis added]'.[16]

In Latin America, the atrocities of Peru's SL rebels are perhaps
most commonly portrayed as senseless. Yet this violence is also the
result of a specific set of historical circumstances. One of SL's major
attractions was its ability to offer social mobility and a leadership
role to young students with few prospects. The teacher-training
programme at the University of Huamanga in Ayacucho produced
many SL militants. Graduates from the programme were generally
limited to badly paid jobs as schoolteachers and were often sent
back to teach in their home villages. The resulting resentment and
frustration appear not only to have made many of these graduates
receptive to SL, but also hostile to the peasantry that they believed
they had left behind.[17] Most of the SL leadership was *mestizo* (mixed-
race), many of whom had been scorned by both *criollo* (descendants
of Spanish settlers) and Indian populations.[18]

More broadly, the desire for improved access to education
seems both to have attracted support to SL, and to have informed
some of the group's more repressive and moralising violence. This
cannot be properly understood in isolation from the racist character
of Peruvian society and the subordination of the Indian population
within it. Carlos Degregori points to the belief among the largely
mestizo officials of the party that 'the masses' had been fooled by their
lack of education into accepting their lot. They must therefore be
indoctrinated into taking a more 'enlightened' path, while at the
same time being coerced into abandoning the vices – alcohol, sexual
licence and tobacco – by which they had allowed themselves to be
deceived. Ironically, given SL's dependence on the drugs trade, coca

consumption was another vice from which the poor needed to be 'weaned'.

In Asia, public humiliation was an important part of the Chinese revolution in 1949 and the Cultural Revolution in 1965–66. Khmer Rouge violence was underpinned by resentment of economically privileged groups in Phnom Penh, many of whom were seen as compounding their sins by collaborating with the US and its bombing campaign.[19] The Khmer Rouge's enthusiasm for forcible 're-education' resembles that of SL.

An aspect of the Bosnian conflict that has often been overlooked is the resentment of many rural Serbs at what were seen as the privileged, middle-class, urban Muslims who owed their position to 'collaboration' with the Ottoman Turks. The war provided the opportunity to avenge this sense of humiliation.[20] The Nazis exploited German shame at the Versailles Treaty and anger at serious economic problems to spread their anti-Semitic message.[21] Hitler had a keen sense of humiliation at the hands of the Jews who he said had laughed at him in Vienna; he vowed that, when he had finished with the Jews, it would be he that was laughing.

Absence of a Revolutionary Ideology

Social and economic exclusion produces grievances that are not necessarily expressed through a disciplined and co-ordinated political or military movement. Even rebellions driven by revolutionary ideology may rely on the rational calculation by peasants that it is in their interest to join.[22] Coherence and a shared political aim appear to depend upon the extent and type of outside help a rebellion receives. During Sudan's first civil war in 1955–72, backing from Israel via Uganda in 1970 helped rebel leader Joseph Lagu to knit together disparate groups into a coherent rebel movement and to negotiate a reasonably favourable peace settlement.[23] During the country's second civil war, which began in 1982, support from Ethiopia was instrumental in uniting southern factions; Mengistu's fall in 1991 re-exposed the SPLA's ethnic origins and fragmented its insurgency.[24]

Levels of political awareness are also significant. In Sierra Leone, the rebels' vision of an alternative society has been poorly expressed, whilst widespread atrocities against civilians have undermined the RUF's credibility as a vehicle for popular political protest. Under-educated recruits, inconsistent foreign support and the lack of a well-developed sense of civil rights have made it difficult for the RUF to carry out disciplined political or military action. Rebels have often preferred violence against unarmed (and often privileged) civilians, which offers more immediate psychological and economic rewards. The lack of well-developed civil institutions such as newspapers and trade unions seems to have contributed to the tendency for grievances to be expressed through decentralised violence that looks like crime, rather than through a coherent political movement. The line between warfare and criminal activity may be neither clear nor rigid.[25] While modern civil wars have commonly moved from political to economic violence, this process can work in reverse. Hobsbawm observes that, while economic crisis and surplus rural populations can encourage banditry, banditry can also spill over into movements with more overtly political aims.[26]

Degree of Impunity

The extent to which ordinary people embrace economic violence depends greatly on the signals that they receive from the political leadership, and the degree to which ordinary people believe they can escape punishment. This will depend in turn on the scale and type of top-down violence. Some degree of impunity is likely to arise from the mere existence of conflict and the breakdown of normal mechanisms for punishing crime.

Not all civil wars create a 'climate of impunity'. Many rebel groups, particularly on the left, have meted out severe punishments for abuse and indiscipline. However, the tendency for civil wars to legitimise abuse appears to be increasing as ideological conflict declines. The absence of mechanisms to punish offenders can encourage human traits that would otherwise be kept in check, such as violent greed or pleasure in exerting power over others. This process can be systematically encouraged: tactics designed to deprive rebel movements of an economic base may call for the dispossession or exploitation of particular ethnic or religious groups.

Official policies such as these may provide fertile ground for violence for private gain. Whether through changes in the law or a growing reluctance to enforce laws, some communities – the *Nuba* and *Dinka* in Sudan in the early 1980s, for example – may find themselves deprived of legal protection, even in peacetime. One of the advantages enjoyed by a government in a civil war is that it alone decides what is legal and what is not.

Although often seen as a sudden catastrophe, the Holocaust followed a gradual erosion of Jews' legal protection throughout the 1930s in Germany. Nazi persecution, while driven primarily by government policy, was enthusiastically supported by parts of German society, sometimes for reasons of professional rivalry or business ambition.[27] As peace turned to war, official and private figures became increasingly interested in the military and economic benefits of

the prosaic benefits of 'ethnic cleansing'

exploiting Jewish labour in the ghettos of Nazi-occupied Europe. This lobby was, however, eventually overcome by advocates of the 'Final Solution'.[28] The prosaic benefits for some of 'ethnic cleansing' in the former Yugoslavia – a house, a television, a fee for transporting victims – are a further reminder that one motive for cooperating with 'ethnic violence' may be the tangible benefits that people expect from it.[29]

In Somalia, official policy has fuelled and licensed private gain. Warfare in the late 1970s and 1980s was usually discussed as a political conflict between the Barre government and rebel groups like the Somali National Movement (SNM), which began armed resistance in northern Somalia in 1981. However, the conflict was exacerbated and shaped by local struggles over trade, land, property and jobs. The SNM revolt gave the government the excuse for widespread and profitable abuse of the *Isaak* clan, which was seen as providing most of the rebels' support. According to a resident of Buroa in northern Somalia:

> *The government deliberately put all the power in the hands of non-*Isaaks. *By 1984 there was no* Isaak *in any position of authority in Buroa ... If an* Isaak *had a business coveted by a non-*Isaak *or which was regarded as a competitive threat, he or she would be labelled a 'trouble maker' and harassed till they got fed up and closed the business – better still, left town.*[30]

In civil wars, envy and greed have repeatedly led to accusations of collaboration with either rebel or government forces (usually whichever is the weaker in a particular region). Local vendettas were common during the 1975–79 revolutionary war in Zimbabwe, for example.[31]

'Bottom-up' violence has many similarities with crime; social and economic exclusion create a powerful motive for securing the immediate wealth and sense of power that crime can bring. But the signals sent out by those in authority are also significant in this context. Is the political or military opposition in a position to channel discontent in an organised and disciplined way? Or is the political establishment able to fracture the opposition by licensing crime and fomenting what appears to be 'chaos'? These political considerations are likely to be critical in determining the extent of economic violence during a civil war.

External Intervention and Economic Violence

This chapter looks at how outside intervention can affect civil wars in which economic agendas play a leading role, and how these conflicts can affect external intervention. Broadly, four main forms of outside intervention can reduce violence:

- emergency aid;
- using or threatening force;
- assisting the development of democracy; and
- reconstruction and development (aid, trade and investment).

If civil wars offer substantial economic benefits to the violent, how is peace ever possible? The costs – including economic costs – will always be an incentive for peace, particularly when they erode political support for rebel movements or bellicose governments. The economic benefits of war may diminish of their own accord, for example when prolonged raiding leaves little left to steal. Peace may be especially likely when a war's declining advantages coincide with its rising costs, particularly if these costs are being borne by politically influential groups.[1] Some analysts have come close to suggesting that the best way to start a peace process is to increase the costs of war by letting it run its course. It would be better, however, to reduce the benefits of violence and increase those of peace.

Civil war is commonly seen in a Manichean light, in which conflict is all things bad (suffering, economic disaster and irrationality) and peace all things good. Yet war has its advantages for some, and peace has its elements of violence for many. Moving from war to peace is likely to represent a realignment of political interests and a readjustment of economic strategies, rather than a clean break from violence to consent, theft to production, or repression to democracy.

If the aim is to prevent conflict in the medium and long term, the question is not only 'how can peace be achieved?', but also 'what kind of peace is desirable – and

war has its advantages for some

realistic?'. What is desirable may not always be realistic; what is realistic may not always be desirable. A peace process will usually involve accommodating the economic interests of rebel leaders. In Cambodia, Ieng Sary, a leading figure in the Khmer Rouge, appears to have struck a deal with the country's two Prime Ministers, Hun Sen and Prince Norodom Ranariddh. Ieng Sary defected from the Khmer Rouge in August 1996. He has received a royal pardon, and he and his troops have been granted continued access to lucrative logging and gem-mining around Pailin near the Thai border.[2] These events were a major blow to the Khmer Rouge, which occupied poorer regions to the north, and to its finances. However, the Ieng Sary deal also appeared to condone violence and corruption. Amnesty International criticised it as contributing to a 'climate of impunity'; an irate King Sihanouk accused both Prime Ministers of competing to 'seduce' Ieng Sary.[3]

Similarly, Palestine Liberation Organisation (PLO) leader Yasser Arafat and the cabal of officials which runs the Palestine Authority (PA) appear to have derived economic benefits from 'peace' with Israel. While Israeli border closures and deepening economic crisis have strengthened militant Palestinian groups such as *Hamas* and *Hizbollah*, members of the leadership have profited from international aid, business monopolies and their ability to move freely to and from Israel. Minister of Civil Affairs Jamil Tarifi has even won contracts to build Israeli settlements.[4]

In Mozambique, a Renamo peace negotiator stated candidly in June 1992 that there is 'no democracy without money'.[5] The peace agreement six months later involved payments of $15m to Renamo by the Italian government. Lonrho made a secret pledge of support to Renamo after its cease-fire. With booty diminishing and foreign aid declining, the deal was a natural consequence for a movement that had consistently extorted protection money from private companies and – in return for 'protecting' the Nacala railway line between Mozambique and Malawi – the Malawian government.[6] In Myanmar, rebellious ethnic groups have signed cease-fire agreements with the military government, the State Peace and Development Council (SPDC), apparently in return for tolerance of drug-trafficking. Khun Sa, who apparently 'surrendered' to the government in January 1996, has reportedly been living unpunished in Yangon, investing in casinos and, most bizarrely, funding a section of the Army.[7]

Cooperation during war may create opportunities for peace, but peace on what basis? Striking the right balance between pragmatism and justice will never be easy.[8] While care must be taken to punish the guilty and to resolve grievances, it is violent men that make peace. Outside intervention must therefore fashion a peace that is more attractive than war for the majority of those involved.

Emergency Aid

Traditionally, emergency aid has been portrayed as a neutral, humanitarian issue distinct from the 'dirty politics' of war. However, crises in the 1990s have shown that aid inevitably affects the politics and economy of war-torn countries and is, in turn, affected by them. The idea of neutral humanitarian relief is premised on the belief that civilian suffering is an incidental result of conflict. However, as the International Committee of the Red Cross (ICRC) and other aid organisations have pointed out, violence in civil wars is increasingly directed specifically against civilians.[9]

Aid has often been provided without detailed analysis of its likely political consequences. Similarly, political obstacles to effective aid distribution, such as the common preference for feeding residents rather than migrants or the use of food as a weapon, have also not been fully addressed. Too often, aid has been designed merely to mop up after a conflict, thereby deflecting attention away from the economic and political processes that underpin violence.

Fuelling Violence?

Although the relationship between emergency aid and violence is complex, it is clear that relief should be designed with its effects on both oppressor and victim in mind. Relief may be a short-term palliative, a distraction, or, worse, may help to fuel violence by becoming part of the political economy that sustains conflict. Typically, this is given scant attention. Aid is delivered to combat zones in a way that often fails to address the causes of the conflict. This partly reflects the peacetime origins of many wartime emergency programmes:

relief aid can fuel violence

> *the relief programmes that one sees in Angola and Somalia usually concentrate on the delivery of basic survival commodities and services. Despite being political emergencies, such programmes have their operational origins in response to floods and droughts.*[10]

The fashion for a speedy shift from relief aid to development while conflict is still under way may make little sense in a protracted crisis, where development will be difficult or impossible and emergency needs may remain considerable.[11] It can also obscure or even assist abuses against the people it is ostensibly trying to help. A UN Development Programme (UNDP) rehabilitation scheme in southern Kordofan, Sudan, was described in 1996 as aiming to 'resettle [returnees] in peace villages and then promote agricultural development to strengthen their attachment to land'.[12] However, the *Nuba*, for whom the scheme was designed, had been forcibly deprived of their land by the Sudanese government, which was trying to concentrate them in these so-called 'peace villages' on the periphery of their territory. The plan therefore suggested either alarming ignorance of, or collusion in, government attempts to dispossess the *Nuba*.[13]

Three circumstances, either individually or together, can increase the risk that emergency aid will contribute to violence and suffering:

1) A counter-insurgency based on depopulating areas of rebel strength and on using relief better to control or monitor civilians from these areas. Emergency relief has been used in this way in East Timor, Ethiopia,

Guatemala, Sudan and Vietnam. The cost of keeping displaced people in government-controlled areas can be one of the main constraints on this kind of counter-insurgency tactic. Aid relief may overcome this restriction.[14] In Sudan, particularly in the late 1980s, famine relief was concentrated on refugee camps in neighbouring Ethiopia and on government garrison towns in the south. This helped Khartoum to depopulate parts of the south, notably oil-rich areas. It also forced civilians to congregate in disease-ridden camps, while giving the SPLA a reason to attack relief shipments.

2) *A major diversion of aid, either before or after it has reached its intended beneficiaries.* Aid can be appropriated directly, through theft, or indirectly, through manipulating exchange rates or contracts for transport, accommodation and protection when major aid operations arrive in a country. Diverting aid intended for the needy is undesirable in itself. In terms of its impact on levels of violence, it carries two dangers. First, it can be an incentive for attacks on civilians, since these typically create the need for aid in the first place. Second, diverted aid can support fighting forces and allow them to rebuild their strength. Aid delivered to Rwandan refugee camps in Zaire in 1994–96 helped *Hutu* militia to regroup, and relief provided for Cambodian refugees in Thailand assisted the rebuilding of the Khmer Rouge after its demise in 1979–80.[15]

Emergency aid may make it easier for factions to attract followers. The UN intervention in Somalia in 1992–95 has been strongly criticised for strengthening the major warlords by increasing their access to resources, for example from rents, security contracts and currency transactions, and by granting them legitimacy, either by negotiating with them or by attacking them. Serb military forces benefited substantially from aid crossing Bosnian Serb territory.[16] Where the UN obtains 'negotiated access' to both sides, as in, for example, Angola and Sudan, aid may boost the fighting capability of each.[17] Gaining access to aid supplies is therefore likely to be an important goal of élites in countries undergoing a protracted civil war. There is a pressing – and commonly neglected – need for effective monitoring of aid supplies.

3) *A lack of international political will to address the root causes of an emergency.* Foreign governments have used the provision of aid as an

excuse for not taking action themselves.[18] Humanitarian operations in Bosnia were sometimes used as an argument against air strikes on Serb forces.[19] Relief operations also seem to have provided an alibi for international inaction in Rwanda – not only the failure to prevent the genocide, but also in the weak efforts to isolate and punish those responsible. Some regimes, in Kenya, Nigeria and Turkey, for example, have used their role in international humanitarian operations to deflect attention from domestic abuses.

Against the argument that emergency aid may fuel violence must be weighed the possibility that it will reduce it. Aid may decrease the 'need' for fighting forces to resort to attacks on civilians. This was the logic behind calls for widespread aid in Somalia in 1991–92, where hunger seemed to be an important factor in persuading young men to join militias. Even when aid is stolen, it can reduce levels of violence by bringing down food prices. Relief operations encourage the presence of aid personnel and journalists in areas where they may witness and publicise acts of violence. This, however, depends on the willingness of aid agencies to speak out. The material conditions in which refugees live are likely to influence their radicalism. Improving these conditions can reduce the appeal of rebel movements and make it more difficult for them to attract recruits.[20]

Getting Aid Through

Delivering aid is likely to be particularly difficult when economic violence has become widespread. Relief supplies may be stolen, resulting in more severe deprivation and, as in Somalia and Sudan, in famine. Secondly, effective relief has sometimes posed a threat to groups benefiting from conflict, for example through reversing or moderating profitable price changes or limiting the number of people fleeing resource-rich areas. Thirdly, many of the conditions suitable to self-enrichment in warfare are themselves likely to pose major obstacles to effective emergency relief. In weak states, poorly paid officials and soldiers will be tempted to steal relief supplies or to block their delivery. Doing so is unlikely to lead to popular calls for punishment under an undemocratic or exclusive regime. Stealing supplies may be particularly attractive to members of a rebel movement with minimal outside financing.

Using or Threatening Force

Peacekeeping operations, private security firms, unilateral or multilateral military intervention, protecting aid operations, controlling the flow of arms and attempting to bring offenders to trial are all examples of the use, or threat, of force. Activities such as these will shape, and be shaped by, the economic processes that accompany a civil war. Using force can make violence less likely by increasing its costs to counter-balance its rewards. This can be done by, for example, threatening judicial procedures against warlords (where this can be made credible). External force can also be used in an attempt to remove the means of inflicting violence. This was the case with the sporadic and ill-fated attempts to disarm Somali militias by the US-led International Task Force from December 1992, and by the later UN Operation in Somalia (UNOSOM).

The personnel and resources deployed as part of an outside force can themselves become an additional source of violence.[21] Underpaid West African Cease-fire Monitoring Group (ECOMOG) troops sold guns to factions in Liberia, for example. The presence of some 23,000 foreign personnel under the auspices of the UN Transitional Authority in Cambodia (UNTAC) in 1992–93 distorted the country's economy and increased social tensions, particularly in Phnom Penh.

The UN peacekeeping operation in Somalia appears to have given a major political and financial boost to the warlords whose actions prompted the initial intervention. Faction leaders benefited from their status as the principal intermediaries with whom the UN dealt.[22] Ken Menkaus and John Prendergast note that in 1993 and 1994:

> *The faction leaders – especially Aideed – greatly benefited from rents, security contracts, employment, currency transactions and a variety of other fringe benefits courtesy of the UNOSOM cash cow. One Somali elder remarked, 'UNOSOM came to save us from the warlords, and ended up aligning with them'.*[23]

According to Menkaus and Prendergast, UNOSOM's greatest failing was to concentrate on promoting 'overly centralized, unsustainable government structures in Mogadishu whose legitimacy came primarily from the barrel of a gun … This greatly exacerbated the conflict, as competing militias positioned themselves for the potential spoils of a new aid-dependent state. In the process, the vast majority of Somalis and their local institutions have been ignored and further marginalized'.[24] UNOSOM's departure eroded the patronage systems of Mogadishu's warlords and reduced the importance of national, as opposed to local, issues. This in turn reduced the 'usefulness' of Mogadishu warlords such as Aideed and Ali Mahdi Mohamed, who had concentrated on these national issues.

During the civil war in Sierra Leone, many chiefs argued that aid agencies and donor organisations were overly concerned with appeasing both sides in the conflict. Repeated attempts to contact the rebel leadership were unsuccessful, and aid supported a government that was encouraging human-rights abuse against civilians. Meanwhile, it was argued, local civil-defence groups that stood up to both government soldiers and rebels were being damagingly neglected. Taking the power of warlords as a given during civil wars may be a mistake. Their influence is not simply possessed, but conferred by their supporters and footsoldiers.

Arms embargoes and disarming warring factions may seem undeniably good policies. However, they too need to be considered in a wider context.[25] Disarming some of Somalia's agricultural clans and urban groups increased their vulnerability to more mobile and herder-based bands. Attempts to collect weapons sometimes simply caused armed men to move to areas that had previously been relatively secure.[26]

Assisting the Development of Democracy

Promoting democracy has been proposed as a way to help to end civil wars, typically with a peace package that includes a plan to hold elections, as in Angola in 1992 and Mozambique two years later. Undemocratic regimes are important factors in fostering economic violence and political rebellion; this suggests an urgent need for international pressure to establish democratic systems in peacetime and, in war, for peace proposals that encourage pluralism. Progress towards democracy is likely to be particularly helpful in reducing the likelihood of violence by lessening social and economic inequalities and minimising criminal impunity among the élite. This underlines the importance of re-forming, rather than simply rebuilding, the state when a civil war ends. It is important that outside involvement helps groups wishing to remould the state in creative and accountable ways.

Democratic government is not, however, a panacea for deeply divided societies, nor does it necessarily halt economic violence: crime is eminently compatible with democracy. The numerous obstacles in the way of establishing democratic government need to be anticipated. Establishing democracy in the West was a long process, and simply holding elections is insufficient. Other steps must be taken: one apparently helpful intervention in Cambodia was the UN's encouragement of local NGOs and the media after the Paris Agreement on a Comprehensive Political Settlement of the Cambodian Conflict of 1991.

Given the economic gains that may be made from war, an election that gives the losers no stake in government may invite further conflict. This was the case in Angola, where UNITA returned to war after losing the 1992 polls; in Rwanda, attempts in 1992–94 to end the civil war by creating a demo-

democratisation needs to be backed financially

cratic government prompted a genocidal backlash from some sections of the *Hutu* élite which stood to suffer from majority politics. To maximise the chances of a successful transition from war to peace, democratisation needs to be backed by financial resources. London-based human-rights NGO African Rights has argued that the international drive towards democratisation in Rwanda ran aground partly because of the resource shortages caused by internationally backed austerity measures.[27]

Democratisation can curtail the role of the military, as in, for example, South Korea, the Philippines, Thailand and Taiwan. But this process needs to be handled with care. It may be important to find ways of making democracy palatable for those in a position to prevent it. This must, however, be weighed against the risk that doing so may make it more difficult to punish those guilty of abuse during conflict. The best response may be to marginalise hardliners by luring their supporters away. Civil wars provide opportunities to attract followers by giving them access to previously unavailable resources. External intervention may do the same, and channelling aid to representative institutions is likely to help them to win the allegiance of potential fighters. Alex de Waal in particular has argued that delivering aid through undemocratic structures can encourage habits of deference and silence that abet violence and make punishment more difficult.[28] In Sierra Leone, groups such as teachers and church workers who might have played a key role in highlighting government soldiers' abuses acquired a stake in the relief system. This seems to have increased their reluctance to speak out.

The challenge is to find legitimate, established sources of authority. These may include local authorities, traditional elders, clan structures and self-defence groups. In states close to collapse, these sources of authority will usually be local, rather than central. It is important that a transition to democracy finds ways to build upon these institutions. As Mark Bradbury notes, 'In wars where the state has collapsed, identifying and working with legitimate civil or political structures must start during the conflict.'[29]

Reconstruction and Development

Trying to address the symptoms and costs of wars without looking at why violence first began may *recreate* the conditions for conflict. Even if it were possible fully to repatriate, reintegrate, rehabilitate and reconstruct, war would simply resume for the same reasons that it initially began.

An alternative model of reconstruction would take better account of the ways in which a society causes violence, rather than assuming that violence is simply superimposed on a society. As with emergency aid, there are dangers in separating wartime violence from its political and economic context. Just as it may be necessary to re-form the state to remove the political and social factors that provoked violence, it may also be necessary to re-form the economy.

Progress is likely to be impeded when aid organisations view war simply as a setback to development processes that are assumed to be benign and to have played no role in causing the conflict. The end of Sudan's first civil war in 1972 did not lead to a more inclusive political system or an economic policy that addressed the problems of the under-developed south. The conditions that caused conflict therefore remained unchanged, and there was no lasting settlement.

To succeed, reconstruction and redevelopment need to address the reasons why people took up arms in the first place.

Top-down Violence

In many countries, colonialism and, later, patterns of international aid and investment reinforced the dominance of particular, often ethnic, groups over others. Because democracy is likely to threaten their position, these élites have used violence to prevent it. When redevelopment or reconstruction aid further bolsters the position of the élite, top-down violence may be made more likely in the long term. On the other hand, a reconstruction programme that offers élites nothing may lead them to undermine a peace settlement.

Weak states play a key role in triggering top-down violence. Reconstruction may therefore need to include propping up their institutions, while at the same time avoiding entrenching the positions of their élite groups. This may mean accepting decentralised government, as in Somalia. This process may, in any case, already be under way. However, the line between recompensing people for stopping violence and rewarding them for having initially engaged in it may be thin. Punishing violence and rewarding peace have distinct policy implications – notably with regard to handling human-rights abuse – that must not simply be glossed over. The immediate post-conflict period can be critical. Amnesty International has noted:

> *Those settlements which have been most successful in protecting human rights have included independent mechanisms for the verification of abuses during the period of implementation of the full provisions of the peace accord, pending the reform or creation of permanent institutions responsible for the protection of human rights.*[30]

Giving or withholding development and reconstruction aid can exert pressure to limit human-rights abuse. This opportunity is, however, frequently missed. In Sudan, international donors pressed the government on its macro-economic policy, but largely ignored the abuses of the militias that Khartoum was arming and controlling. In El Salvador, the US, the World Bank and the IMF have all made it clear that assistance is linked to acceptable economic policy, but have not pushed through more sensitive initiatives such as land reform with similar vigour. In 1996, after the huge international peacekeeping effort in Cambodia in 1992–94, the country received almost half of its $410m budget from Western countries. Few

ignoring human-rights abuse and focusing on macro-economic policy

conditions were attached to these funds: donors largely ignored their responsibilities under the Paris peace agreement to link assistance with applying the rule of law. This omission appears to have increased authoritarianism and corruption.[31] In 1996, with the IMF and World Bank voicing concerns about corruption and lack of government revenue, aid was temporarily suspended.

War may make easier some types of economic activity such as raiding or trading in scarce commodities. Peace, on the other hand, may assist others, such as industry, agriculture and normal trade. The art of a successful transition from war to peace may lie in ensuring that at least some of those benefiting from war will benefit more from peace. In practical terms, at least initially, this may mean an 'armed peace' in which influential figures remain able to affect economic activity by threatening to return to war.[32] Groups that have used violence to gain control of production, trade and emergency aid in wartime may retain some of this influence in peace. Mafia-type groups in Somalia have benefited from the degree of order established as conflict abated.[33] Companies set up by UNITA have negotiated diamond-mining concessions with a view to peacetime exploitation. Part of the point of wartime violence may be precisely to secure a lucrative position within the peacetime economy. It can be argued that only the most naked exploitation, such as massive theft of assets from particular groups, is impossible in peacetime.

Bottom-up Violence

NGOs that claim to address the apparent root causes of conflict by tackling poverty risk giving inadequate attention to top-down violence, where diplomatic pressures may offer the best solution. The increasing involvement of Western aid ministries in conflict-resolution presents a similar danger. Nonetheless, addressing the needs of ordinary people is important. The rebellion in Sierra Leone was partly the result of the country's poor social services and education system. The government's inability to meet the material, educational and security needs of its population encouraged young men to join rebel and government forces, using their access to weaponry and their near-immunity from prosecution to steal from civilians and to protect themselves.

Ordinary people can turn to violence for economic gain, to defend themselves from economic loss, or to ensure their physical security. The common distinction in the media and aid-agency literature between 'innocent civilians' and 'men of violence' obscures the frequency with which civilians have taken up arms as members of militias, government forces or rebel groups. Aid may have to address the needs of these combatants as well as of their victims. If reconstruction aims simply to recreate the political economy that existed when war began, it is unlikely to do so. Intervention must therefore establish alternative ways of ensuring physical and economic security to weaken the appeal of warlords, extremist politicians and faction leaders. In Peru, part of SL's appeal lay in its ability to protect peasants from criminals, drug-traffickers, the police and US-backed coca-eradication programmes. The government's most effective counter-insurgency strategy has been to offer an alternative source of protection by minimising harassment of the peasantry and promising that new crops would be substituted for coca, as well as striking against SL guerrillas directly. Firm action against traffickers lowered the price of coca, making crop substitution more attractive. Conversely, repression and heavy-handed coca eradication have been counter-productive, as has failure to deliver on crop-substitution pledges.

Intervention aimed at achieving quick economic growth, rather than addressing inequality, may make renewed conflict more likely.[34] Unequal land distribution is at the root of conflicts in Central America.[35] El Salvador's ex-combatants have seen only limited, and badly delayed, land transfers after peace accords in 1992; there have also been delays in establishing a civil police force (called for in the peace accords) and in purging the Army officer corps. Taxation remains regressive, crime rates have risen and organised violence threatens to resume.[36] Part of the problem appears to have been the rigid division of responsibilities between international agencies, with the World Bank and IMF handling economic reconstruction – which has made macro-economic reform a priority – and the UN supervising the peace process itself.

Although democratisation may lead eventually to a fairer distribution of resources, international financial institutions have only weakly backed political and judicial reform in El Salvador. These institutions appear to have exerted more substantial pressure for reform in Guatemala. This seems to have pushed through important policy reforms: improving health and education services; providing cheap credit to allow the poor to buy some land; and reducing military spending and the size of the armed forces. Nonetheless, land reform remains a contentious issue.

The widespread sale of land to foreign interests, notably Portuguese, South African and Zimbabwean, after the end of Mozambique's civil war could threaten peace by further harming a peasantry that has already suffered under colonialism, Frelimo's socialist collectivisation and as a result of war and famine.[37] There is a risk that war could be replaced by continual high crime rates and that former Renamo fighters could turn against a leadership perceived to have betrayed its original aims.[38]

Finally, it may be difficult to demobilise soldiers after a war unless they are offered incentives that offset the benefits of fighting.[39] Economic incentives must be used to secure support for the peace process from fighters being demobilised and integrated into a new army. In Angola in 1992, many demobilised fighters who had been neither paid nor fed deserted and turned to crime.[40] Funding demobilisation may not be easy, particularly when a government lacks access to resources. Demobilisation in Liberia has been difficult partly because warlords deprived the government in Monrovia of revenues from timber, minerals and iron ore. Foreign funding can fill these gaps.[41]

Demobilisation programmes, particularly in Africa, have often assumed that soldiers will 'return' to the land. However, not all soldiers are former farmers; many who were may have turned to violence precisely because farming offered them few rewards. Many of those who took part in the Renamo insurrection in Mozambique did so in protest at government schemes to force people into rural areas. The dislocations of warfare may have bred a preference for urban, rather than rural, living.[42] According to General João de Matos, the Angolan Army Chief-of-Staff,

> *a soldier with 12 or 15 years in the army is not a farm*
> *worker. He will immediately sell the kit, then spend the*
> *money, wasting it because he has no experience of budgeting*
> *for himself – in two weeks he's a potential bandit.*[43]

Much of the discussion of reconstruction and development aid, particularly the dangers of recreating pre-war economic conditions through reconstruction and development aid also apply to trade and investment issues. Foreign trade and investment may be a powerful incentive for governments to abide by international norms. Many countries are keen to gain access to international trading blocs; an acceptable human-rights record may make this easier. On the other hand, foreign investment and trade can also increase human-rights abuse by, for example, encouraging a regime to displace people from resource-rich areas. This process has a long history: the growing demand for agricultural produce in industrialising England, for example, helped

the dangers of recreating pre-war economic conditions

to fuel the evictions and famine in Ireland in the 1840s. The depopulation of Somalia's Jubba and Shabeelle areas that caused the 1992 famine was partly a response to the opportunities offered by foreign investment, notably in the banana industry.[44] In Cambodia, Liberia and Myanmar, foreign interest in timber and valuable minerals has fuelled economic violence. Ellis noted in 1996 that Liberia was a

> *theatre of conflict between various French-speaking elites,*
> *notably in Abidjan, Ouagadougou and Conakry, and*
> *powerful factions in Nigeria, aspiring to regional hegemony.*
> *Rival warlords in Liberia secure resources inside the country*
> *which they then trade with external allies in return for*
> *weapons, using the associated trade flows and capital to*
> *build a domestic clientele and to capture slaves.*[45]

Menkaus and Prendergast draw an important lesson that is applicable beyond Somalia when they note that 'Under no conditions should donors and NGOs assist in major agricultural projects if land has been usurped by force from original owners. The international community has a special responsibility to safeguard the rights of minority agricultural communities, and not to legitimise the military occupation of land by outsiders'.[46]

Funds flowing out of a country can also influence patterns of violence. Regulating these investments, and perhaps freezing the assets of élites held abroad, may be a way of discouraging them from conflict. Charles King suggests that the Colombian government's decision to freeze guerrilla bank accounts and confiscate their assets seems to have been more effective than direct military attacks.[47]

Dilemmas for Outsiders

Both top-down and bottom-up violence stand in the way of efforts to prevent and resolve conflict. This presents a major problem for outside agencies: if economic and social problems are not tackled, bottom-up violence will remain a strong possibility; but addressing these tensions may prompt top-down violence in the form of a backlash by endangered élites. A parallel dilemma confronts those keen to punish human-rights abuse and remove 'impunity'. These problems are not insoluble, and a pragmatic approach may be more helpful than calls for an 'end to impunity' or a 'climate of forgiveness'. Amnesty International appears increasingly to accept that, if human-rights abuse is fully acknowledged, it may not be necessary to insist on punishment in every case.

Outside intervention is not simply a form of surgery to 'remove the warlords', an 'injection' of emergency aid or troops or a one-off 'prescription' of democracy. Rather, it should aim to assist processes already under way. Thinking clearly about the dilemmas involved will require looking hard at the complex and varied functions of violence.

conclusion

This paper does not argue that *all* civil wars are dominated by economic agendas, but that a combination of factors has given these agendas new importance in many contemporary conflicts. Although post-Cold War optimists have suggested that capitalism, peace and democracy are natural bedfellows, this paper gives grounds for caution. It is true that there has been a major push for democracy in many countries. But the backlash from those threatened by pluralism has often been terrible. It is true that communist support for rebel movements has declined and that increasing numbers of politicians subscribe to free-enterprise economics. But free enterprise has frequently taken violent forms, and increased economic violence has often filled the vacuum left by the loss of external support.

Those attempting to ease the suffering caused by civil wars, or to address conflict's root causes, must understand that stereotyping conflict as a result of ancient ethnic hatreds, as breakdown or as a struggle between two sides is inadequate and can obscure the reasons why civil wars continue. For the embattled élites of weak states, provoking economic violence is an affordable way to fight rebels and to suppress more general political opposition. Valuable resources in areas of conflict can encourage the emergence of war economies in apparently chaotic situations. Social and economic exclusion, the decline of socialism or communism and weak political organisation have made ordinary people more susceptible to calls for ethnic or economic violence. Although political struggles have not disappeared, contemporary civil wars have often encouraged crime, rather than revolution. Under these conditions, peace is not always what it appears. Understanding what can be gained from war may allow policy-makers to create incentives that make violence less attractive, and therefore less likely.

If outside involvement in a civil war is to succeed in mitigating its effects, it must take into account the political and economic interests of the violent. The old model in which civilians are seen as hapless victims of conflict may be less appropriate than one that sees them as its intended targets. For emergency aid to reach its destination, the interests of those who benefit from theft and famine prices must be addressed. This may include:

- a more widespread distribution of aid to reduce the incentive to steal it;
- closer monitoring;
- diplomatic pressure to resolve problems with delivery and distribution; and
- consistent donor support for NGOs in conflict with those impeding relief.

Major donors and UN agencies are not sufficiently concerned with what happens to their aid after they have dispatched it. Closer attention to this issue would encourage donors and the UN to tackle economic and political manipulation of crises and the human-rights abuses that usually underpin humanitarian emergencies. There has been a marked reluctance to do this in many countries, particularly where no special rapporteur on human rights has been appointed.

If outside involvement is to succeed in making violence less likely, it must take into account the ways in which it could actually *increase* violence by magnifying its benefits. Even the psychological functions of violence need to be understood in terms of the political economy present when war began. The interests of those who can benefit from violence need to be taken seriously, otherwise opportunities to influence the violent will continue to be missed. External interventions that focus on the victims and the instigators of violence are likely to be more cost-effective and more successful than those that focus on victims alone.

This paper suggests no easy answers. Outside intervention is unlikely in itself to end a civil war, but it can have an important impact. Effective involvement will lessen the benefits of violence and reduce moral and legal impunity. This can be achieved by providing realistic economic alternatives to violence, both for those at the top and those at the bottom of a social hierarchy, and by creating the means to punish abuse and exploitation by all combatants, not just the 'rebels'. This means monitoring abusive groups more carefully and publicising their activities more widely. It is also important that assistance is linked explicitly with human-rights observance, rather than with a package of conditions, including structural adjustment. This bundling together of conditions tends to dilute the message that the international community may wish to convey. Targeting leaders by denying them access to foreign bank accounts and overseas travel can also give important leverage.

At the same time, it will be important to find ways to avoid a backlash from those threatened by an end to hostilities. This means handling democratic transitions and the introduction of free markets with a sensitivity that has sometimes been lacking. To address bottom-up violence, outside involvement will need to meet the needs of civilians. These may be a lack of economic or educational opportunities or physical security. This is likely to mean strengthening and improving – rather than dismantling or bypassing – the institutions of the state, such as schools, social-security systems and, in many instances, establishing a more accountable police force and Army.

Since the end of the Cold War, NGOs have sought to become increasingly involved in resolving conflicts, rather than simply in alleviating their effects. These organisations often claim a comparative advantage over governments in this area gained through their development work at the grassroots. While many NGOs are well placed to comment on the links between deprivation and bottom-up violence, they may be less able to influence top-down violence because they lack the diplomatic weight of governments. Conflict theorists and this new breed of NGOs, such as the London-based International Alert, have portrayed conflict either as a misunderstanding, to be resolved through talks, or as a political struggle needing a negotiated settlement. Both views assume that all sides in a civil war share an interest in ending it, even though they favour different kinds of peace. By contrast, this paper argues that 'opposing' parties may have a shared interest in war. This need not, however, make peace impossible. The 'war aims' of the parties may be surprisingly similar: to stay alive; to experience more power and excitement than seems possible in peacetime; and, perhaps above all, to benefit economically. The key is to build societies in which these shared aims can be achieved through peace, rather than war. There is an urgent need to concentrate not only on the 'causes' of war, but also on the many functions of violence. One critical step forward would be improvements in the international monitoring and understanding of attempts to manipulate decisions in civil society through using militias and encouraging economic violence.

Internal Conflicts, 1994–98

Country	Principal Participants	Date	Status
Afghanistan	*Taleban*, factions led by Burhannudin Rabbani and Abdul Rashid Dostum	1992–	Active[a]
Albania	Government (G), northern opposition	1997	Cease-fire March 1997[b]
Algeria	G, *Front Islamique de Salut* (FIS), GIA	1992–	Active
Angola	G, UNITA	1975–94	Peace accord signed with UNITA November 1994[c]
Azerbaijan	G, 'Republic of Nagorno-Karabakh'	1992–94	Cease-fire signed May 1994, but no comprehensive settlement
Bangladesh	G, *Shanti Bahini* (Chittagong) guerrillas	1982–97	Cease-fire signed December 1997
Bosnia	G, Croat and Serb forces	1992–95	General Framework Agreement for Peace in Bosnia-Herzegovina (the Dayton Accords) signed December 1995; implementation problems continue
Burundi	G, Front for the Defence of Democracy (FDD)	1993–	Active
Cambodia	G, remnants of Khmer Rouge	1997–	Active
Central African Republic	G, Army rebels	1996–98	Bangui Accords signed March 1998
Chad	G, *Comité de Sursaut National pour la Paix et la Démocratie* (CSNPD), other factions	1980–94	Peace accord. CSNPD splinter group *Forces Armées de la République Fédérale* (FARF) resumed violence October 1997

appendix

Country	Principal Participants	Date	Status
Colombia	G, FARC, ELN	1963–	Active
Comoros	G, *Anjouan* separatists	1997	Cease-fire
Congo	Forces led by President Pascal Lissouba, former President Denis Sassou-Nguessou	1997	Cease-fire
Croatia	G, Serbs	1991–95	'Basic Agreement' between local Serb community and Croatian government reached November 1995; UN troops remain in disputed areas of Prevlaka and Eastern Slavonia
Cyprus	G, Turkish and Turkish Cypriot forces	1974	*De facto* cease-fire between Cyprus National Guard and Turkish and Turkish Cypriot forces in place since 1974
Georgia	G, 'Republic of Abkhazia', South Ossetia	1992–94	Cease-fire signed with Abkhaz separatists July 1993, but no comprehensive settlement
Guatemala	G, URNG	1968–96	Cease-fire and peace accord signed December 1996
Haiti	*Lavalas, Forces Armées d'Haiti* (FADH)	1991–95	Peace accord September 1994
India	G, Kashmiri separatists	1989–	Active
Indonesia	G, FRETILIN, Irian Jaya factions	1975–	Active
Iran	G, Kurdish Democratic Party of Iran (KDPI), 1979–, *Mujahidin-e-Khalq* (Me–K)		Active

Country	Principal Participants	Date	Status
Iraq	G, Kurdish factions in south	1988–	Active
Israel	G, PLO, *Hamas, Hizbollah*, other factions	1948–	*Hamas* and *Hizbollah* activity continues following Oslo Accords between Israel and the PLO in 1993
Lebanon	G, *Hizbollah*, South Lebanon Army (SLA)	1978–	Active (Israel's self-declared 'security zone' in the south)
Liberia	G, National Patriotic Front (NPF), *Krahn* factions	1989–96	Peace accord
Mali	G, *Tuareg, Mouvements et Fronts Unifiés de l'Azouad* (MFUA)	1989–94	Peace accord
Mexico	G, *Ejército Zapatista de Liberación Nacional* (EZLN)	1994–	Several rounds of peace talks since April 1995, but no conclusive settlement
Moldova	G, Transdniestr separatists	1992–94	Peace accord
Mozambique	G, Renamo	1976–95	General Peace Agreement signed 1992
Myanmar	G, Karen National Union (KNU), National Coalition Government of the Union of Burma (NCGUB), other factions	1985–	Active
Nicaragua	G, *Frente Norte* (FN) 380, remnants of Contras	1982–95	Peace accord signed February 1994

Country	Principal Participants	Date	Status
Niger	G, *Front Démocratique de Renouveau* (FDR), *Co-ordination de la Résistance Armée* (CRA), *Organisation de la Résistance Armée* (ORA)	1991–96	Peace accords signed April 1995, October 1997
Papua New Guinea	G, Bougainville Revolutionary Army (BRA)	1988–98	Cease-fire signed April 1998
Peru	G, SL, MRTA	1981–	Active
Philippines	G, Moro National Liberation Front (MNLF), Moro Islamic Liberation Front (MILF), New People's Army (NPA)	1969–	Peace accord with MNLF signed September 1996
Russia	G, Chechen separatists	1994–96	Peace accord signed August 1996, but no comprehensive settlement on status of Chechnya within Russian Federation
Rwanda	Rwandan Patriotic Army (RPA), Rwandan Armed Forces (FAR), *Interahamwe* militia	1990–	Active
Senegal	G, *Mouvement des Forces Démocratiques de la Casamance* (MFDC)	1997–	Active
Sierra Leone	G, RUF	1991–	Active
Somalia	Factions formerly led by Hussein Aideed, Ali Mahdi Mohamed, others	1991–	Active
Sri Lanka	G, Liberation Tigers of Tamil Eelam (LTTE)	1983–	Active
Sudan	G, SPLA	1983–	Active

Country	Principal Participants	Date	Status
Tajikistan	G, Islamic Movement of Tajikistan (IMT), other factions	1992–96	Cease-fire signed December 1996
Turkey	G, PKK	1984–	Active
Uganda	G, Lord's Resistance Army (LRA), other factions	1985–	Active
UK	G, Republican, Unionist groups	1969–	'Good Friday' Agreement signed April 1998, but no comprehensive settlement
Western Sahara	G, *Frente Popular para la Liberación de Saguia el-Hamra y de Río de Oro* (POLISARIO)	1975–	Formal cease-fire in place since September 1991, but no comprehensive settlement
Yemen	G, breakaway 'Democratic Republic of Yemen'	1994	Secessionists defeated mid-1994
Yugoslavia (Federal Republic)	G, Kosovo Liberation Army (UCK)	1997–	Active
Zaire/DROC	G, ADFL	1996–97	ADFL ousted President Mobutu Sese Seko May 1997

Notes   [a] Active: covers current conflicts which may vary from low-intensity (or intermittent) encounters to high-intensity (or constant) combat; [b] Cease-fire: agreed by recognised leaders of disputants, but does not stand as a resolution of the conflict. Does not suggest that all conflict has stopped; [c] Peace accord: formal resolution of conflict ratified by recognised leaders of disputants. In some cases, not all conflict may have ended

Sources   'The Status of Armed Conflict 1994–1997' wallmap in *The Military Balance 1997/98* (Oxford: Oxford University Press for the IISS, 1997); Charles King, *Ending Civil Wars*, Adelphi Paper 308 (Oxford: Oxford University Press for the IISS, 1997), pp. 84–87

notes

Acknowledgments

The author would like to thank
Mats Berdal, Rose Gottemoeller,
David Shearer, Lawrence Tal and
Michael Williams for their
encouragement and advice.
Additional research for the
Appendix by Hilary Kivitz.

Introduction

[1] Keith Somerville, 'Angola –
Groping Towards Peace or
Slipping Back Towards War?', in
William Gutteridge and Jack
Spence (eds), *Violence in Southern
Africa* (London: Frank Cass, 1997),
p. 27; Margaret Anstee, *Orphan of
the Cold War: The Inside Story of the
Collapse of the Angolan Peace
Process, 1992–93* (Basingstoke,
Hants: Macmillan Press, 1996);
Mats Berdal, *Disarmament and
Demobilisation after Civil Wars:
Arms, Soldiers and the Termination
of Armed Conflict*, Adelphi Paper
303 (Oxford: Oxford University
Press for the IISS, 1996).
[2] Mark Duffield, *Complex Political
Emergencies: With Reference to
Angola and Bosnia – An Exploratory
Report for UNICEF* (Birmingham:
University of Birmingham Press,
1994); Berdal, *Disarmament and
Demobilisation after Civil Wars*.
[3] *Ibid.*, pp. 20–30.
[4] See, for example, Hans Magnus
Enzensberger, *Civil Wars* (London:
Granta, 1994).
[5] While civil wars were never
simply a 'theatre' for Cold War
rivalries, superpower
involvement and the importance
of 'ideology' obscured the role of
internal forces in shaping conflict.
See Tim Allen, 'International
Interventions in War Zones', in
Tim Allen, Kate Hudson and Jean
Seaton (eds), *War, Ethnicity and the
Media* (London: South Bank
University Press, 1996), pp. 7–22.
[6] See, for example, Robert D.
Kaplan, *Balkan Ghosts: A Journey
Through History* (New York:
Vintage Books, 1994), which is
sometimes seen as influential in
persuading US President Bill
Clinton's administration that
nothing could be done to end
hostilities in the former

Yugoslavia. See also Kaplan, 'The Coming Anarchy', *Atlantic Monthly*, vol. 275, no. 2, February 1994, pp. 44–76; Daniel Patrick Moynihan, *Pandaemonium: Ethnicity in International Politics* (Oxford: Oxford University Press, 1993); and Martin van Creveld, *The Transformation of War* (New York: The Free Press, 1991).
[7] David Keen, 'Organised Chaos Not the New World We Ordered', *World Today*, January 1996, pp. 14–17; Charles King, *Ending Civil Wars*, Adelphi Paper 308 (Oxford: Oxford University Press for the IISS, 1997), pp. 25–28.

Chapter 1

[1] See A. Rangasami, 'Failure of Exchange Entitlements' Theory of Famine: A Response', *Economic and Political Weekly*, vol. 20, no. 41, October 1996.
[2] See, for example, A. V. B. Norman, *The Medieval Soldier* (New York: Barnes and Noble, 1971), p. 23; Philippe Contamine, *War in the Middle Ages* (Oxford: Blackwell, 1986), p. 219; and Charles Tilly, 'Routine Conflicts and Peasant Rebellions in Seventeenth Century France', in Robert P. Weller and Scott E. Guggenheim (eds), *Power and Protest in the Countryside: Studies of Rural Unrest in Asia, Europe, and Latin America* (Durham, NC: Duke University Press, 1982).
[3] David E. Stannard, *American Holocaust: Colombus and the Conquest of the New World* (Oxford: Oxford University Press, 1992), pp. 213–14.
[4] See David Keen, *The Kurds in Iraq: How Safe is Their Haven Now?* (London: Save the Children Fund, 1993), p. 28.

[5] Alex Vines, *Renamo: From Terrorism to Democracy in Mozambique* (London: James Currey, 1996), p. 140.
[6] See David Keen, *The Benefits of Famine: A Political Economy of Famine and Relief in Southwestern Sudan, 1983–89* (Princeton, NJ: Princeton University Press, 1994), pp. 109–12.
[7] See Ken Menkaus and John Prendergast, *Political Economy of Post-intervention Somalia*, Somalia Task Force Issue Paper No. 3, April 1995, p. 15; and Alex de Waal, *Famine Crimes: Politics and the Disaster Relief Industry in Africa* (London: James Currey, 1997), pp. 159–78.
[8] See, for example, Manuel Pastor and James K. Boyce, *The Political Economy of Complex Humanitarian Emergencies: Lessons from El Salvador*, WIDER Working Paper No. 131 (Helsinki: World Institute for Development Economics Research (WIDER), 1997), pp. 1–44.
[9] See Guenter Lewy, 'Some Political–Military Lessons of the Vietnam War', in Lloyd J. Matthews and Dale E. Brown (eds), *Assessing the Vietnam War: A Collection from the Journal of the US Army War College* (Washington DC: Brassey's, 1987), pp. 142–44. Although loss of support from the US Congress in 1973–74 created shortages of equipment and ammunition and lowered morale in the South Vietnamese armed forces, the military's internal weakness would alone probably have led to defeat.
[10] David P. Chandler, *The Tragedy of Cambodian History: Politics, War and Revolution Since 1945* (New Haven, CT and London: Yale University Press, 1991), pp. 192–235.

[11] William Shawcross, *Sideshow: Kissinger, Nixon and the Destruction of Cambodia* (London: André Deutsch, 1979), especially Chapters 11, 12 and 14.

[12] Mats Berdal and David Keen, 'Violence and Economic Agendas in Civil Wars', *Millennium*, vol. 26, no. 3, 1997, pp. 804–805.

[13] William Shawcross, 'Tragedy in Cambodia', *New York Review of Books*, 14 November 1996, pp. 43–44.

[14] *Ibid.*

[15] John Aglionby, 'Timorese Find Little to Cheer', *The Guardian*, 17 July 1996, p. 13.

[16] African Rights, *Components of a Lasting Peace in Sudan: First Thoughts*, Discussion Paper No. 2 (London: African Rights, 1993), p. 10.

[17] Information on Sierra Leone comes primarily from the author's fieldwork in June–July 1995. See also Mark Bradbury, *Rebels Without a Cause? An Exploratory Report on the Conflict in Sierra Leone* (London: CARE, 1995).

[18] Stephen Ellis, 'Liberia 1989–1994: A Study in Ethnic and Spiritual Violence', *African Affairs*, vol. 94, no. 375, April 1995, pp. 165–97.

[19] Tom Porteous, 'A Glimpse of Hell', *The Spectator*, 7 October 1995, pp. 18–20.

[20] Berdal and Keen, 'Violence and Economic Agendas in Civil Wars'.

[21] Carlotta Gall and Thomas de Waal, *Chechnya: A Small Victorious War* (London and Basingstoke, Hants: Pan Books, 1997), pp. 240–41.

[22] Phil Gunson, 'The End may be Near for Guatemala's Long War', *The Guardian*, 27 March 1996, p. 14.

[23] John Simpson, *In the Forests of the Night: Encounters in Peru with Terrorism, Drug-running and Military Oppression* (London: Arrow Books, 1994), pp. 185–87.

[24] *Ibid.*, p. 188.

[25] *Ibid.*

[26] Patrick L. Clawson and Rennselaer W. Lee, *The Andean Cocaine Industry* (London: Macmillan, 1996), p. 183.

[27] See, for example, Lewy, 'Some Political–Military Lessons of the Vietnam War', p. 45, on US mistakes in Vietnam.

[28] See, for example, Anthony Joes, *Guerrilla Conflict before the Cold War* (Westport, CT: Praeger, 1996); and Paul Schulte, *Interrogating Pontecorvo: The Continuing Significance and Evolving Meanings of 'The Battle of Algiers'* (London: Royal College of Defence Studies, 1996), p. 45.

[29] On military tactics and economic benefits surrounding the Kurdish conflict, see Kemal Kirişçi and Gareth M. Winrow, *The Kurdish Question and Turkey: An Example of a Trans-State Ethnic Conflict* (Ilford, Essex: Frank Cass, 1997), pp. 126–33.

Chapter 2

[1] Michael Ignatieff, *Blood and Belonging: Journeys into the New Nationalism* (London: BBC Books/Chatto & Windus, 1993), p. 16. See also Keen, *The Benefits of Famine*, especially Chapters 2 and 3.

[2] On Mozambique, see Vines, *Renamo*, p. 99; and William Finnegan, *A Complicated War: The Harrowing of Mozambique* (Berkeley, CA: University of California Press, 1992), pp. 224, 227.

[3] Norman, *The Medieval Soldier*, pp. 252–57.

[4] Alex de Waal, 'Land Tenure, the Creation of Famine and Prospects

for Peace in Somalia', in M. A. Mohamed Salih and Lennart Wohlgemuth (eds), *Crisis Management and the Politics of Reconciliation in Somalia* (Uppsala: Nordiska Afrikainstitutet, 1994), pp. 40–41.

[5] Eric J. Hobsbawm, *Bandits* (London: Weidenfeld & Nicolson, 1969), p. 89.

[6] Interview in Freetown, Sierra Leone, June 1995.

[7] *Ibid.*

[8] *Ibid.*, June–July 1995.

[9] In Chechnya, troops often feared their own officers. See Gall and de Waal, *Chechnya*, p. 237.

[10] Bishop W. Nah Dixon, *Great Lessons of the Liberian Civil War, and What Did We Learn? A Personal View* (Monrovia: Feed My People, 1992).

[11] An impoverished Mozambican Army also carried out abuses against civilians. See Human Rights Watch, *Conspicuous Destruction: War, Famine and the Reform Process in Mozambique* (Washington DC: Human Rights Watch, 1992).

[12] Vines, *Renamo*, pp. 95–100, 143.

[13] See Lara Marlowe, 'Axemen Rule in Algeria's Killing Fields', *The Observer*, 8 December 1996, p. 18.

[14] De Waal, *Famine Crimes*, pp. 161.

[15] Ronald E. Robinson and J. Gallagher, *Africa and the Victorians* (London: Macmillan, 1961).

[16] Conrad Russell, *The Crisis of Parliaments: English History, 1509–1660* (Oxford: Oxford University Press, 1971), pp. 378–79.

[17] Martin van Bruinessen, *Aghaa, Shaikh and State: The Social and Political Structures of Kurdistan* (London: Zed Books, 1992), pp. 185–86.

[18] Stephen Ellis, 'Analysing Africa's Wars', *Anthropology in Action*, vol.

3, no. 3, Winter 1996, p. 18.

[19] William Reno, 'The Business of War in Liberia', *Current History*, vol. 95, no. 601, May 1996, pp. 212–13.

[20] See, for example, George Klay Kieh, 'Combatants, Patrons, Peacemakers and the Liberian Civil Conflict', *Studies in Conflict and Terrorism*, vol. 15, no. 2, April 1992, p. 130.

[21] Somerville, 'Angola – Groping Towards Peace or Slipping Back Towards War?', pp. 34–36.

[22] Hobsbawm, *Bandits*, p. 91.

[23] Federico Varese, 'Is Sicily the Future of Russia? Private Protection and the Rise of the Russian Mafia', *Archives Européenes de Sociologie*, vol. 35, no. 2, 1994, p. 249.

[24] Gall and de Waal, *Chechnya*, pp. 124–36; 'Russia's Military: The Politics of Reform', IISS, *Strategic Comments*, vol. 2, no. 8, October 1996.

[25] Varese, 'Is Sicily the Future of Russia?', pp. 224–58.

[26] David Shearer, *Private Armies and Military Intervention*, Adelphi Paper 316 (Oxford: Oxford University Press for the IISS, 1998), pp. 40–42.

[27] *Ibid.*, p. 51.

[28] Menkaus and Prendergast, *Political Economy of Post-intervention Somalia*, p. 6.

[29] Clawson and Lee, *The Andean Cocaine Industry*, pp. 189–91.

[30] Jenny Pearce, *Colombia: Inside the Labyrinth* (London: Latin American Bureau, 1990), p. 262.

[31] On counter-insurgency in particular, see Joes, *Guerrilla Conflict before the Cold War*.

[32] Francois Jean and Jean-Christophe Rufin (eds), *Economie des Guerres Civiles* (Paris: Hachette, 1996).

[33] This process is evident in Sierra

Leone. See Paul Richards, 'Rebellion in Liberia and Sierra Leone: A Crisis of Youth?', in Oliver Furley (ed.), *Conflict in Africa* (London: I. B. Tauris, 1995), pp. 134–70; and Paul Richards, *Fighting for the Rainforest: War, Youth and Resources in Sierra Leone* (London: Heinemann, 1996).

34 Vines, *Renamo*, pp. 20–26, 89–90.

35 Somerville, 'Angola – Groping Towards Peace or Slipping Back Towards War?', pp. 22–23.

36 Clawson and Lee, *The Andean Cocaine Industry*, p. 190.

37 See, for example, Thomas T. Vogel, 'Middle Ground: Despite Guerrillas, Business Marches on in Colombian Jungle', *Wall Street Journal*, 16 March 1998, pp. 1, 5.

38 Clawson and Lee, *The Andean Cocaine Industry*, pp. 186.

39 Sarita Kendall, 'Colombia Measures the Cost of Violence', *Financial Times*, 11 November 1996, p. 9.

40 Clawson and Lee, *The Andean Cocaine Industry*, p. 180.

41 Kieh, 'Combatants, Patrons, Peacemakers and the Liberian Civil Conflict', p. 131.

42 See, for example, K. B. Wilson and J. Nunes, 'Repatriation to Mozambique', in Tim Allen and Hubert Morsink (eds), *When Refugees Go Home: African Experiences* (London: James Currey, 1994), p. 179; Vines, *Renamo*, pp. 88–94.

43 Jean-Christophe Rufin, 'Les Economies de Guerre dans les Conflits Internes', in Jean and Rufin (eds), *Economies des Guerres Civiles*, pp. 19–59.

44 François Jean, 'The Plight of the World's Refugees at the Crossroads of Protection', in Julia Groenewold (ed.), *World in Crisis: The Politics of Survival at the End of the Twentieth Century* (London: Routledge, 1997), pp. 42–57.

45 See, for example, Alex de Waal, 'The Shadow Economy', *Africa Report*, March–April 1993, pp. 24–28.

46 African Rights, *Rwanda: Death, Despair and Defiance* (London: African Rights, 1994), especially Chapters 1 and 2; and Gerard Prunier, *The Rwanda Crisis, 1959–1994: History of a Genocide* (London: Hurst and Company, 1995), especially Chapters 5, 6 and 7; René Lemarchand, 'Rwanda: The Rationality of Genocide', in Obi Igwara (ed.), *Ethnic Hatred: Genocide in Rwanda* (London: ASEN Publications, 1995), pp. 59–70.

47 Enoch Opondo, 'Representation of Ethnic Conflict in the Kenyan Media', in Allen, Hudson and Seaton (eds), *War, Ethnicity and the Media*, pp. 133–151.

48 Charles Maechling, 'Counterinsurgency: The First Ordeal by Fire', in Michael T. Klare and Peter Kornbluh, *Low-intensity Warfare: Counterinsurgency, Proinsurgency, and Antiterrorism in the Eighties* (New York: Pantheon, 1988), p. 44.

49 Pearce, *Colombia: Inside the Labyrinth*.

50 Robert Fox, 'Algeria's Trail of Blood Leads to the Armed Forces', *Sunday Telegraph*, 26 October 1997.

51 David Hirst, 'Escalation of Blood', *The Guardian*, 25 September 1997, p. 17; 'The Killing Suburbs of Algiers', *ibid.*, 21 October 1997, p. 12; John Sweeney, 'We Accuse. 80,000 Times', *The Observer*, 16 November 1997, p. 33.

52 Menkaus and Prendergast, *Political Economy of Post-intervention Somalia*, p. 9.

53 Clawson and Lee, *The Andean Cocaine Industry*, pp. 179–82, 191.

[54] Kendall, 'Colombia Measures the Cost of Violence'.
[55] Gerhard Dilger, 'Mauss Trap Slams Shut', *The Guardian*, 27 November 1996, p. 23.
[56] Hobsbawn, *Bandits*, pp. 84–85, 90.
[57] See, for example, Susan L. Woodward, *Balkan Tragedy: Chaos and Dissolution After the Cold War* (Washington DC: Brookings Institution, 1995), pp. 289–94; Julian Borger, 'Saddam's Elite Rides High Despite UN Sanctions', *The Guardian*, 3 March 1998, p. 12.
[58] See, for example, Mark Duffield, 'The Political Economics of Internal War: Asset Transfer, Complex Emergencies and International Aid', in Joanna Macrae, Anthony Zwi, Hugo Slim and Mark Duffield (eds), *War and Hunger: Rethinking International Responses to Complex Emergencies* (London: Zed Books, 1996), pp. 50–69.

Chapter 3

[1] Contamine, *War in the Middle Ages*, pp. 243–44.
[2] *Ibid.*, p. 244.
[3] Norman, *The Medieval Soldier*, pp. 168–69.
[4] Mark Chingono, *The State, Violence and Development: The Political Economy of War in Mozambique, 1975–1992* (Aldershot, Hants: Avebury, 1996).
[5] Clawson and Lee, *The Andean Cocaine Industry*, pp. 185–88.
[6] *Ibid.*, p. 180.
[7] Hobsbawm, *Bandits*, p. 65.
[8] Interview in Freetown, Sierra Leone, June 1995.
[9] Interview in Bo, Sierra Leone, June 1995.
[10] Vines, *Renamo*, p. 116.
[11] Robert Malley, *The Call from Algeria: Third Worldism, Revolution and the Turn to Islam* (Berkeley, CA: University of California Press, 1996), p. 126.
[12] Schulte, *Interrogating Pontecorvo*, p. 39.
[13] Frantz Fanon, *The Wretched of the Earth* (New York: Grove Press, 1986), p. 74, cited in Schulte, *Interrogating Pontecorvo*, p. 41.
[14] Hobsbawm, *Bandits*, pp. 64–65.
[15] Paul Richards, 'Violence as Cultural Creativity: Social Exclusion and Environmental Damage in Sierra Leone', Department of Anthropology, University College London, 1996, pp. 6, 13.
[16] Interview in Bo, Sierra Leone, June 1995.
[17] Ton de Wit and Vera Gianotten, 'The Origins and Logic of Shining Path', in David Scott Palmer (ed.), *The Shining Path of Peru* (London: Hurst and Company, 1992), pp. 51–52.
[18] Carlos Ivan Degregori, 'The Maturation of a Cosmocrat and the Building of a Discourse Community: The Case of the Shining Path', in David Apter (ed.), *The Legitimization of Violence* (Basingstoke, Hants: Macmillan/ United Nations Research Institute for Social Development, 1997), p. 54.
[19] See, for example, Ben Kiernan, *The Pol Pot Regime: Race, Power and Genocide in Cambodia Under the Khmer Rouge, 1975–79* (New Haven, CT: Yale University Press, 1996).
[20] Peter Maass, *Love Thy Neighbour: A Story of War* (Basingstoke, Hants: Papermac, 1996), pp. 52–53.
[21] See, for example, Thomas J. Scheff, *Bloody Revenge: Emotions, Nationalism and War* (Boulder, CO: Westview Press, 1994), pp. 105–24.
[22] Samuel Popkin, *The Rational*

Peasant: The Political Economy of
Rural Society in Vietnam (Berkeley,
CA and London: University of
California Press, 1979).
[23] See, for example, Douglas H.
Johnson and Gerard Prunier, 'The
Foundation and Expansion of the
Sudan People's Liberation Army',
in M. W. Daly and Ahmad Alawad
Sikainga (eds), *Civil War in the
Sudan* (London: British Academic
Press, 1993), pp. 117–41.
[24] African Rights, *Components of a
Lasting Peace in Sudan*, pp. 7–8.
[25] See van Creveld, *The
Transformation of War*.
[26] Hobsbawm, *Bandits*, especially
Chapters 6, 7.
[27] Michael Burleigh and Wolfgang
Wippermann, *The Racial State:
Germany 1933–1945* (Cambridge:
Cambridge University Press,
1991), p. 86.
[28] Christopher Browning, *The Path
to Genocide: Essays on Launching
the Final Solution* (Cambridge:
Cambridge University Press,
1995), especially Chapters 2 and 3.
[29] See, for example, Maass, *Love
Thy Neighbour*, pp. 76–78.
[30] Africa Watch, *Somalia: A
Government at War with its own
People* (New York, Washington DC
and London: Africa Watch, 1990),
p. 117.
[31] Norma J. Kriger, *Zimbabwe's
Guerrilla War* (Cambridge:
Cambridge University Press,
1992).

Chapter 4

[1] David Keen, *The Political Economy
of War* (Oxford: Queen Elizabeth
House, 1996), pp. 22–24.
[2] Shawcross, 'Tragedy in
Cambodia', pp. 41–46; and William
Shawcross, 'The Cambodian
Tragedy, Cont'd', *New York Review*

of Books, 19 December 1996, pp.
73–74. Hun Sen himself defected
from the Khmer Rouge before
becoming Foreign Minister and
then Prime Minister under the
Vietnamese from 1978.
[3] Shawcross, 'Tragedy in
Cambodia', p. 45.
[4] David Hirst, 'Shameless in Gaza',
The Guardian, 21 April 1997, pp.
8–10.
[5] Vines, *Renamo*, p. 145.
[6] *Ibid.*, pp. 145–47.
[7] Nick Cumming-Bruce, 'Junta
"Aids Heroin Trade"', *The
Guardian*, 27 November 1996,
p. 14.
[8] For a good discussion of this
dilemma, see King, *Ending Civil
Wars*, pp. 61, 65.
[9] See, for example, Human Rights
Watch, *Evil Days: 30 Years of War
and Famine in Ethiopia* (New York
and London: Human Rights
Watch, 1991), pp. 13, 16. On the
increasing civilian death-toll in
twentieth-century conflicts, see
Eric Hobsbawm, *The Age of
Extremes: A History of the World,
1914–1991* (London: Vintage
Books, 1996), pp. 49–52. Violence
against civilians is not, of course, a
new phenomenon. English
Commissary-General Henry
Ireton pursued a crop-burning
and starvation policy when faced
with the threat of an Irish alliance
with Charles II in 1649. See
Russell, *The Crisis of Parliaments*,
pp. 385–86.
[10] Duffield, *Complex Political
Emergencies*, p. 4.
[11] Ataul Karim, Mark Duffield et
al., *OLS (Operation Lifeline Sudan):
A Review* (Birmingham: University
of Birmingham, 1996), pp. 7–11;
Duffield, *Complex Political
Emergencies*, p. 3.
[12] Karim, Duffield et al., *OLS
(Operation Lifeline Sudan)*, p. 217.

13 *Ibid.*; African Rights, *Facing Genocide: The Nuba of Sudan* (London: African Rights, 1995), pp. 1–9.

14 David Keen and Ken Wilson, 'Engaging with Violence: A Reassessment of Relief in Wartime', in Macrae, Zwi, Slim and Duffield (eds), *War and Hunger*, pp. 209–221.

15 William Shawcross, *The Quality of Mercy: Cambodia, Holocaust and Modern Conscience* (London: André Deutsch, 1984), especially Chapter 17.

16 Duffield, *Complex Political Emergencies*, p. 62.

17 *Ibid.*, p. 42.

18 See, for example, Adam Roberts, *Humanitarian Action in War*, Adelphi Paper 305 (Oxford: Oxford University Press for the IISS, 1996).

19 See, for example, Woodward, *Balkan Tragedy*, p. 297.

20 Liisa Malkki, *Purity and Exile* (Chicago, IL: Chicago University Press, 1995).

21 See, for example, Reno, 'The Business of War in Liberia', pp. 213–15.

22 African Rights, *Operation Restore Hope, A Preliminary Assessment* (London: African Rights, 1993), pp. 29–35.

23 Menkaus and Prendergast, *Political Economy of Post-intervention Somalia*, p. 15.

24 *Ibid.*, p. 16.

25 Berdal, *Disarmament and Demobilisation after Civil Wars*.

26 See, for example, *Operation Restore Hope*, pp. 22–27.

27 African Rights, *Rwanda*, pp. 21–22.

28 See de Waal, *Famine Crimes*, pp. 213–21.

29 Mark Bradbury, *Aid Under Fire: Redefining Relief and Development Assistance in Unstable Situations*, Wilton Park Paper 104 (London: Her Majesty's Stationery Office, 1995), p. 15.

30 Amnesty International, *Sierra Leone: Towards a Future Founded on Human Rights* (London: Amnesty International, 1996).

31 Shawcross, 'Tragedy in Cambodia', p. 45.

32 Compare Charles Tilly, 'War-making and State-making as Organised Crime', in Peter Evans (ed.), *Bringing the State Back In* (Cambridge: Cambridge University Press, 1985), pp. 169–91.

33 Menkaus and Prendergast, *Political Economy of Post-intervention Somalia*, pp. 11–12.

34 Pastor and Boyce, *The Political Economy of Complex Humanitarian Emergencies*, pp. 1–44. See also Berdal, *Disarmament and Demobilisation after Civil Wars*, p. 73.

35 See Tom Barry, *Roots of Rebellion: Land and Hunger in Central America* (Boston, MA: South End Press, 1987).

36 Pastor and Boyce, *The Political Economy of Complex Humanitarian Emergencies*, pp. 1–44.

37 Chris Alden, 'Political Violence in Mozambique', in Gutteridge and Spence (eds), *Violence in Southern Africa*, pp. 52–55.

38 *Ibid.*, p. 55; Vines, *Renamo*, pp. 152–63.

39 See Berdal, *Disarmament and Demobilisation after Civil Wars*.

40 Somerville, 'Angola – Groping Towards Peace or Slipping Back Towards War?', p. 28.

41 Max Ahmadu Sesay, 'Bringing Peace to Liberia', in Jeremy Armon and Andy Carl (eds), *The Liberian Peace Process, 1990–1996* (London: Conciliation Resources, 1996), pp. 77–78.

42 Chingono, *The State, Violence and Development*; and Vines,

Renamo, p. 163.

[43] General João de Matos quoted in Victoria Brittain, 'Angola Faces Chaos as Soldiers Return to Soil', *The Guardian*, 12 June 1996, p. 14.

[44] De Waal, 'Land Tenure, the Creation of Famine and Prospects for Peace in Somalia', p. 31.

[45] Ellis, 'Analysing Africa's Wars', p. 19.

[46] Menkaus and Prendergast, *Political Economy of Post-intervention Somalia*, p. 17.

[47] King, *Ending Civil Wars*, p. 68.